Basic Dictations

Catherine Sadow
Judy DeFilippo

PRO LINGUA  ASSOCIATES

Pro Lingua Associates, Publishers
P.O. Box 1348, Brattleboro, Vermont 05302 USA
Office: 802-257-7779, Orders: 800-366-4775
Email: info@ProLinguaAssociates.com
WebStore: www.ProLinguaAssociates.com
SAN: 216-0579

*At **Pro Lingua***
our objective is to foster an approach
to learning and teaching that we call
***interplay**, the **inter**action of language*
learners and teachers with their materials,
with the language and culture,
and with each other in active, creative,
*and productive **play**.*

Copyright © 2013 by Catherine Sadow and Judy DeFilippo

ISBN 13: 978-0-86647-347-7 – 10: 0-86647-347-5

Basic Dictations was designed by Arthur A. Burrows. It was set in Palatino, the most widely used, and pirated, face of the twentieth century, which was designed by Hermann Zapf in 1948 in Frankfurt. Although modern, it is based on Renaissance designs typical of the Palatinate area in Germany.

The photographs illustrating this book are from Dreamstime.com Agency, except as noted:
p. 1 Jen © Vincent Giordano, p. 1 Ben © Hugo Maes, p. 2 Liz © Andres Rodriguez, p. 3 Joe © Jose Antonio Nicoli, Anna © Andres Rodriguez, Lisa © Andres Rodriguez, Tom © António Jorge Da Silva Nunes, p. 4 Brad Pitt kids © Jolie/Pitt family, p. 5 Jack © Anna Lurye, Pam © Dundamin, Donald © Robert Kneschke, Jan © Katseyephoto, Bob © Tonylivingstone, Mike © Robert Lerich, Lisa © Lucian Coman, Lee © Toxawww, Nick © Khorzhevska, Amy © Wxin, Jim © Nyul, Ted © Olga Sapegina, Susan © Valua Vitaly, Alan © Nyul, Jay © Surabky, Jenna © Olga Sapegina, p. 6 left © Yarek Gora, center © Aprescindere, right © Dmitriy Shironosov, p. 8 cocker © Boomfeed, p. 8 Boston Terrier © Radomír Režný, p. 17 penny, quarter © Atu Studio, nickel © Kbiros, dime © Karen Struthers, bills © Cammeraydave, p. 23, 25, 27 clocks © Richard Thomas, p. 25, 26 © Vania Dobrinova, p. 27 map © Kaarsten, p. 27 calendar © Rasà Messina Francesca, p. 31 winter © Nyul, spring © Ikatyusha, summer © Louis Capeloto, fall © Richard Gunion, p. 32 map © Tangducminh, weather symbols © Gheburaseye, p. 34 flag girl © Lafleur312, p. 35 Washington © Georgios, p. 35 Lincoln © Jose Gil, p. 36 blouse © Evaletova, shirt © Evaletova, hat © Gemenacom, pants © Gsermek, back pack © Norman Pogson, shoes, belt © Raja Rc, jacket © Lepas, dress © Evgeniy_p, tie © Felinda, boots © Elena Butinova, scarf © Le-thuy Do, gloves © Francesco Alessi, stockings © Jimmyi23, sweater © Aliaksei Asipovich, bra © Gordana Sermek, skirt © Kadrof, p. sale © Ariwasabi, p. 38 sweater © Moony2009, tie © Vicente Barcelo Varona, tee © Gemenacom, jacket © Stratum, shirt © Tombaky, p. 39 Sam © Fotoskat, p. 40 big table © Ales Borut Ivanko, Small table © Anton Starikov, double bed © Lesuhova, twin bed © Andrea Leone, sofa © Bonsa, easy chair © Olga Naidenova, washer © Oleg Shelomentsev, refrigerator © Cemil Adakale, stove © Margojh, bookcase © Katya Triling, mirror © Mishkacz, towel © Jack14, rag rug © Olena Chyrko, oriental rug © Irina Veremeenko, pot © Volodymyr Khotenko, pan © Empire331, frying pan © Andrea Leone, lamp © Andrea Leone, dishes © Costasz, pillows © Karam Miri, living room © Ijansempoi, bathroom © Jjayo, kitchen © Susan Leggett, bedroom © Irina88w, p. 41, 42 Chen © Monkey Business Images, p. 56 cigarette © Abel Tumik, p. 57 recycling © sunsetman, p. 58 fruit © The Big Book of Art, p. 59 scale © Suprijono Suharjoto, p. 61 shopper, list © Andres Rodriguez, Melinda Fawver, p. 64 meat, bread © Daniel Hurst, fruit © Mihail Syarov, vegetable © Tyler Olson, milk © Og-vision, p. 68 couple © Eastwest Imaging, p. 69 body parts © Valua Vitaly, pp. 69, 70 Henry © Aliced, p. 73 blood pressure © Radu Sebastian, p. 74 stethoscope © Sylwia Kucharska, p. 75 internal organs © Judy DeFilippo based on an illustration in Lifeskills, 2nd Ed./Pearson is 1991, p. 78 mouth © Alila07, tooth brush © Chimpinski, floss © Cammeraydave, toothpaste © Milosluz, p. 81 baby brushing © Ziprashantzi, p. 82 baby sleeping © Liumangtiger, p. 84 needle © Jpldesigns, p. 85 vaccine © Dmitry Naumov, p. 86 teacher © Ron Chapple, doctors © Nyul, police © Lisa F. Young, mechanic © Tyler Olson, plumber © Kurhan, rocker © Artur Gabrysiak, hair stylist © Brian Chase, pilot © Typhoonski, 90 register © Lisa F. Young, bus © Py2000, nurse's aide © Lisa F. Young, baker © Otnaydur, electrician © Lisa F. Young, 100 banker © Pemotret, auto parts © Judy DeFilippo based on an illustration in Lifeskills, 2nd Ed./Pearson is 1991, p. 78 car © Dbrus, car crash © John Takai, Barbara © Andres Rodriguez. Forms on pages 77, 92-93, 95, 98-99, 111 are government forms in the public domain or based on such forms. The standard road signs on pages 113-115 are also in the public domain. *Cover:* photo © Matthewjade, design A. A. Burrows.

The book was printed and bound by McNaughton & Gunn in Saline, Michigan.

Printed in the United States of America.

First edition, second printing 2013. 1,200 copies in print.

Other Pro Lingua books by Catherine Sadow
and Judy DeFilippo

Great Dictations
High-Beginning to Low-Intermediate

Interactive Dictations
Intermediate

Dictations for Discussion
Intermediate to Advanced

Also from Pro Lingua

Dictation Riddles

Acknowledgements

The authors based many of their activities on concepts introduced by P. Davis and M. Rinvolucri, who co-authored *Dictation, New Methods, New Possibilities*, Cambridge University Press.

The dictations in this book are original texts, not quoted from other sources. However, they are based on extensive research in various internet sources. The authors are grateful to the authors and publishers whose insights, information, facts, and figures are used in many of our dictations. Three articles from the internet were the major sources for three of our original dictations, of the same titles. These are "Eat Right!" "Fifty Minutes on the Road." and "How Much Do They Make?"

Contents

Introduction

Friends and Families

Numbers

Time

Note: *L* indicates Additional Listening Activities - see page vii.

Around Town

Food

Health

Work

Introduction

Basic Dictations is a mid- to high-beginning level text that is intended to improve the listening and speaking skills of ESL students. Reading and writing skills are also reinforced, along with attention to vocabulary and grammar. This text provides a variety of dictation topics that are useful for newcomers living in the United States.

The text is photocopyable, and units are designed to stand alone so that teachers can pick and choose which dictations meet the needs, interests, and levels of their students. Each unit begins with a short introduction that provides a background and context for the dictation. The introduction is followed by a short list of vocabulary items whose meanings are central to the dictation. The list also provides a chance to hear the teacher pronounce these important vocabulary items and to have the students repeat them. The central focus of the unit is a dictation activity. In some chapters there is an additional listening activity. Each dictation / listening is followed by a discussion section. The discussions can take place in pairs or small groups. With some units, the teacher may want to discuss the issues with the whole class.

The units in this text are one, two, or three pages long. Therefore, some units will take less time than others. A shorter unit or part of a unit can be done as a fill-in. The dictation and discussion times will vary depending on the level of the class.

The complete texts of the dictations begin on page 117. These full texts can be read to the students, or a student can read them to the class. The complete texts are also available on a CD. On the first page of each unit, there is a *Teacher's note* in the margin giving the CD track and the location of the complete dictation text and of the explanation of how to give the dictation.

❋ Different Types of Dictations ❋

Through the years, dictation has been presented in many forms in reading, listening, grammar, and writing classes. It is also used as an assessment procedure. This text, however, does not deal with scoring or analyzing student work. The dictations are meant to be a challenging springboard to discussion in which the students are encouraged to use the language they have just encountered in the dictation. This text includes four forms of dictation: partial, pair, dictogloss, and prediction.

In this text, the direction lines are minimal. It may be necessary to supplement them with your own directions in the first few units you do. The rest of this introduction fully explains what you need to know.

1. Partial (sometimes known as *cloze*)

Most of the dictations in this text are partial dictations where words, phrases, or chunks of language have been deleted, and students are required to listen and write down the missing words. All the dictations should be discussed upon completion. Pair work is encouraged, and spelling can be corrected at the time of completion.

2. **Pair** (sometimes known as *mutual*)

This dictation requires students to work in pairs to combine two partial texts into one continuous piece. One student (Student A) has a gapped copy of the dictation, and the other student (Student B) has a different gapped copy. Each student has half of the text. They should not look at each other's texts. Student A dictates and Student B writes, then B dictates and A writes, back and forth, and so on until the story is complete. The first one the students do should be modeled first.

3. Dictogloss

In this kind of dictation, the focus is on getting the gist or main idea of a sentence.

Students are told that they will hear a sentence only once, after which they are to jot down the words they can recall and try to reconstruct the sentence in writing as accurately as they can. The first time this is done, the teacher will probably have to allow the students a second reading until they discover that they need to pay attention the first time around. This is especially true for beginning-level students. As the students work at rebuilding the sentences, they can work in pairs or groups of three or four. Some teachers like to have students write their sentences on the board for all to see, correct, and discuss.

4. Prediction

Prediction lessons come in two parts. The first part focuses more on reading skills and grammar. The students can work individually or in pairs, reading the passage and predicting (or guessing) what should be in each blank space. Any logical or grammatically correct word or phrase can be accepted. The second part requires the students to listen to the same passage and see if their guesses were correct, or similar.

Additional Listening Activities

Seventeen of the units in this text have listening sections. After the dictation, there are short conversations that recycle the vocabulary in the dictations. There are exercises and activities that follow these conversations in each unit.

Students should listen first and try to do the activity. They can listen as many times as they need to. For a follow-up activity, the teacher might give the students the complete text of the conversation and have them read it aloud.

Also, in several chapters there are charts to fill in. These are not dictations but practice in listening and writing down the information requested. See page 21 as an example.

Introduction ❀

❀ Tips for Teachers ❀

1. When reading the full dictations, try to speak naturally, at normal speed, keeping the features of the spoken language. If you are reading the full text at normal speed and you know the exercise will be fairly easy for your students, give the word, phrase, or chunk of language only once. Try to start with a pace that is comfortable for your students, and then make them work a bit at understanding. If you think the text will be difficult for your students, repeat it once or possibly twice. When we were field testing our material, several teachers said they thought the material looked quite difficult for their students, but they were surprised at how well their students did. It's up to you to decide what works best. If you have to repeat it more than three times, the text is too difficult for your students.

2. The students may want to check the spelling of a word or words as you are giving the dictation. It's best to tell them to wait until the end of the activity.

3. For single-digit numbers (1-9), have the students write the words (two rather than 2). For larger numbers, have the students write numerals, rather than the word (15 instead of fifteen). They should also use dollar ($) and percentage (%) symbols rather than writing out the words.

4. One key to making the dictation a positive experience is to have students correct their own work. When the dictation is completed, the students in pairs check with each other on what they've heard, while you walk around helping and clarifying. This in itself allows for a great deal of discussion. After they have self-corrected, they can turn to the full dictation texts for confirmation. You can then go over the dictation with the class and discuss whatever vocabulary or concepts they don't understand.

5. Rather than read the full dictations, you may find it helpful to copy the page you're dictating and fill in the blanks ahead of time. This is helpful when giving your students feedback. It's easier when you're working from the same page as your students. Here is an example from the Trivia Contest chapter:

   On *what* *date* do Americans celebrate Valentine's Day?

   What does *9/11* stand for?

6. There is no single pattern that was followed when choosing words or phrases to be deleted. Sometimes the deletions focus on idioms, sometimes on numbers, sometimes grammar, sometimes vocabulary.

7. *Basic Dictations* also works well for substitute teachers, since a minimum amount of preparation is needed.

8. You and your students can also create dictations from local newspapers, the Internet, or any other source. This way you can choose a timely topic and easily adapt it to the level of your students.

9. Discussions. The discussion can be in pairs, small groups, or the entire class. In some units there are two discussions. They can be done in any order. To save time, one can be eliminated.

❀ Pronunciation ❀

When introducing the vocabulary, you may want to ask students to repeat some of the words or phrases after you introduce them. Students often know the meaning of a word but are afraid to use it because they don't know what it sounds like. They'll probably need to use some of the words in the discussion that follows the dictation and will feel freer to use them if they have already said them aloud.

❀ Using the CD ❀

On the CD, each dictation text or listening conversation is on a separate track. The CD track numbers are given in the table of contents, beneath the titles of the gapped texts, and next to the page numbers of the full dictation texts.

Although it is not necessary to have and use the accompanying CD, many teachers find that having the CD provides greater flexibility in using the material. For example, when students are listening to conversations between two or more people, the CD can be much more effective than the teacher reading both parts. Below are suggestions for using the CD:

❀   Play the track once through without stopping, before reading the dictation to the students. This will introduce the topic and give the students a head start toward comprehending the dictation when it is read to them.

❀   To give the students a chance to hear a different voice, have the students take the dictation from the CD. Although more challenging, this can help students prepare for standardized listening tests. You can use the pause button; that will allow the students time to fill in the blanks.

❀   Play the CD after the students have taken the dictation and checked their answers. This can help students improve and become more confident in listening comprehension.

Introduction ❀

❀ Using a Listening Laboratory ❀

Almost any dictation that is done in class can also be done in the listening lab. However, there are additional things that can be done in the lab that cannot be done in a classroom.

1. Read a short and easy partial dictation in the lab. The dictation can be from this text or something you have devised on your own. Then have the students record what they have written. You can collect both, and then on the student CD, give them some feedback on their pronunciation. If they can do this successfully, next time make the dictation a little longer.

2. Dictate a problem. An example might be a "Dear Abby" letter that you have turned into a dictation (or try one of the Abby-type letters in this text). After each student has done the dictation, they record the solution to the problem. You should listen and respond to the solution, or the students can move from station to station to listen to their fellow students and make comments of agreement or disagreement. By preparing short, easy-to-understand dictations first, you can also use this technique to introduce other survival or cultural topics that you think will be of particular interest to your students.

❀ About the Full Dictation Texts ❀

The complete texts for the dictations begin on page 117. You can read these full texts to give the dictations.

Basic
Dictations

What Is Your Name?

Teacher's note:
CD track 1
Full text 117
Instructions
for doing the
dictation:
page 116

Introduction

Let's talk about people's names. Answer these questions.

Jen

What is her name? *Her name is Jen.*

Ben

What is his name? _____.

What is your name? _____.
What is your first name? _____.
What is your last (family) name? _____.

Partial Dictation

Listen and write the words you hear in the blank spaces. Check your answers with a partner.

My English Class

Hello. My _____ is Ji Young. I _____ from South Korea. In my

English _____ there are students from different countries. Ken ____ from

Japan, Rosa is _____ Mexico. Ahmed and Khalid _____ from Iraq. Ozzie

____ from Turkey. We are ____ small class. _____ are friends.

Discussion

Work with a partner and answer these questions. Share your answers with the class.

1. Is Ji Young from South Korea?   Yes, she is.
2. Is Rosa from South Korea?   No, she isn't. She's from Mexico.
3. Is Ken from Japan?
4. Is Ji Young from Japan?
5. Is Rosa from Mexico?
6. Are Ahmed and Khalid from Iraq?
7. Are you from Iraq?
8. Is your name Rosa?
9. Where are you from?

Basic Dictations © 2013 Catherine Sadow and Judy DeFilippo

What's Your Nickname?

Teacher's note:
CD track 2
Full text 117
Instuctions
for doing the
dictation:
page 116

Introduction

Here are some formal names and some nicknames. Match the names in Column A with the nicknames in Column B.

A		B	
1.	Robert	a.	Kathy, Kate
2.	James	b.	Betsy, Libby, Lizzie
3.	Katherine	c.	Bob, Bobby, Rob
4.	Susan	d.	Jimmy, Jim
5.	Elizabeth	e.	Billy, Bill, Will
6.	William	f.	Sue, Suzy

Partial Dictation - Listen and fill in the blank spaces.

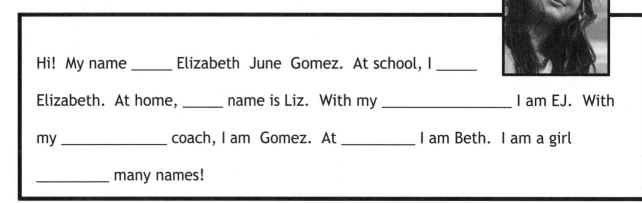

Hi! My name _____ Elizabeth June Gomez. At school, I _____ Elizabeth. At home, _____ name is Liz. With my _____ I am EJ. With my _____ coach, I am Gomez. At _____ I am Beth. I am a girl _____ many names!

Discussion

1. What's her name with _____?
   a. her math teacher   b. her mother   c. her sister   d. her friend Maria
   e. her coach   f. her principal   g. her boss   h. her father

2. The story is mostly about Elizabeth and _____.
   a. her family   b. her teachers   c. her names   d. her friends

3. Some nicknames are different from the person's name. Can you match column A with Column B?

A		B	
1.	a red-haired person	a.	Shorty
2.	a thin person	b.	Doc
3.	a doctor	c.	Red
4.	a short person	d.	Skinny Minni

The Garcia Family

Teacher's note:
CD track 3
Full text 117
Instuctions
for doing the
dictation:
page 116

Introduction

The Garcia family is an immigrant family from Mexico. They live in California now.

Vocabulary and Pronunciation

1. **immigrant**: a person who comes to a country to live permanently
2. **single**: not married
3. **divorce**: a legal ending of a marriage
4. **widowed**: a person whose husband or wife has died

Partial Dictation - Listen and fill in the blank spaces.

Joe **Anna** **Lisa** **Tom**

The Garcia family _____ _____ San Diego, California.

Joe and Anna _____ married. Joe is _____

husband. Anna is Joe's wife. Joe _____ Anna are

parents _____ _____ children, Tom and Lisa. Tom is

_____ son, and Lisa_____ their daughter. Anna

is Lisa and Tom's _____. Joe is Lisa and Tom's

_____. Joe and Anna are U.S. citizens

_____. They came _____ Mexico in 2001.

Discussion 1

Practice asking each other yes/no questions. Here are some examples:

1. Is Joe married?
2. Is Joe the wife?
3.
4.
5.
6.

Discussion 2

With a partner, talk about your families.

1. Parents? Brothers and sisters?
2. Married? Single? Divorced? Widowed?

Basic Dictations © 2013 Catherine Sadow and Judy DeFilippo

The Jolie-Pitt Family

*Teacher's note:
CD track 4
Full text 117
Instuctions
for doing the
dictation:
page 116*

Introduction

Angelina Jolie and Brad Pitt are famous movie actors and parents. What do you know about them?

Vocabulary and Pronunciation

1. **adopt**: to take legal responsibility for acting as parents of a child
2. **humanitarian**: a person devoted to finding a better life for all people
3. **biological child**: born to the mother, not adopted
4. **partner**: person who joins together with one or more people for a common goal
5. **twins**: two children born to the same mother at the same time

Partial Dictation - Listen and fill in the blank spaces.

Angelina Jolie is a famous _____ actress, writer, _____ director. She is

also famous _____ _____ her humanitarian work _____third world

countries. She and _____ partner, actor Brad Pitt, have _____ children.

Three are adopted: Maddox (born in _____) is from Cambodia, Pax (2003)

_____ _____ Vietnam, and Zahara (_____) is from Ethiopia. Brad and

Angelina have three biological_____: a daughter, Shiloh (2006), and

_____Knox and Vivienne, born _____ _____.

Discussion 1

With a partner, finish the sentences any way you like. There are different possible answers.

1. Angelina Jolie is
2. Brad Pitt is
3. Maddox is
4. Pax is

5. Zahara is
6. Shiloh is
7. Knox and Vivienne are

Discussion 2

With a partner, talk about these families.

1. A family you know who has adopted children
2. A family you know who has twins (identical or fraternal)
3. A family you know who has children from different countries.

Ted's Family

Teacher's note: CD track 5 Full text 118 Instuctions for doing the dictation: page 116

Introduction/Vocabulary/Pronunciation

Here are the members of Ted's family. Practice saying the words.

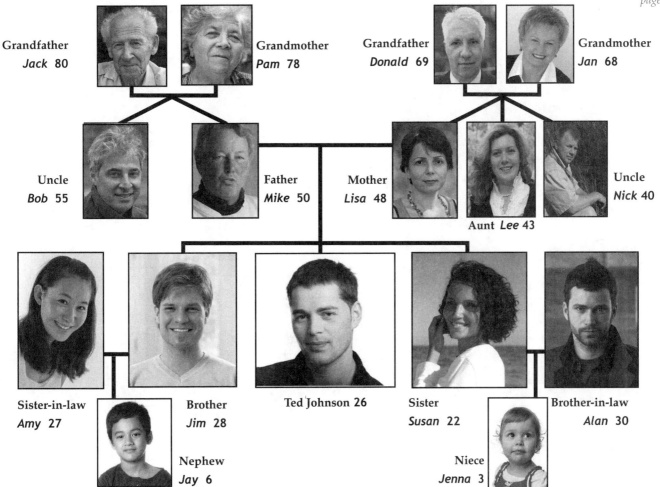

Grandfather *Jack* 80 — Grandmother *Pam* 78 — Grandfather *Donald* 69 — Grandmother *Jan* 68

Uncle *Bob* 55 — Father *Mike* 50 — Mother *Lisa* 48 — Aunt *Lee* 43 — Uncle *Nick* 40

Sister-in-law *Amy* 27 — Brother *Jim* 28 — Ted Johnson 26 — Sister *Susan* 22 — Brother-in-law *Alan* 30

Nephew *Jay* 6 — Niece *Jenna* 3

Partial Dictation

Listen and write the word you hear in the blank space. Then write "yes" or "no" next to the number.

_____ 1. Ted Johnson is _____ _____ _____.

_____ 2. His _____ name is Jim.

_____ 3. His brother Jim _____ _____ _____Susan.

_____ 4. Ted's _____is 58 years old.

_____ 5. Ted's _____is Amy.

_____ 6. Ted's _____are Mike and Lisa.

_____ 7. Ted has_____ _____.

_____ 8. Jenna is Ted's _____

Dictation, continued

_____ 9. Ted's_____, Mike, has a _____, Bob.

_____ 10. Is Jay Ted's_____?

_____ 11. Is Lisa _____ _____?

_____ 12. Lisa and Lee _____ _____.

_____ 13. Ted has_____ _____.

_____ 14. Jenna and Jay _____ _____.

_____ 15. Ted's _____ are Lisa and Amy.

Discussion, Part 1

With a partner, explain each person's relationship to Ted. The first one is done for you. Remember the possessive mark.

Susan	*She's Ted's sister.*	
Mike		
Lee	Pam	Alan
Jan	Bob	Amy

Discussion, Part 2

Talk about your family and your ideas.

Talk about your brothers/sisters/ aunts/uncles/nephews/nieces.
Is your family big or small? (A large American family today is 5 children.)
What is a good age to get married? For a man? woman?
What is a "close" family?

Word Practice

Circle the word that does not belong.

family, mother, father, sister

father, grandfather, aunt, uncle

aunt, sister, married, niece,

son-in-law, brother-in-law, mother-in-law, mother

Amy, Lisa, Lee, Susan

Jay, Bob, Jenna, Pam

My New Family

Teacher's note:
CD track 6
Full text 118
Instuctions for doing the dictation: page 116

Introduction

An older man is not happy about things children are doing. He needs some advice.

Vocabulary and Pronunciation

1. **widow**: a woman whose husband has died
2. **widower**: a man whose wife has died
3. **son-in-law**: the man who is married to your daughter
4. **iPhone**: a phone you can do many things with
5. **rude**: not polite

Partial Dictation - Listen and fill in the blank spaces.

Dear Friend,

I am _____ years old. My first wife is dead. Now I am married to a widow, and _____ _____ _____ very much. We are _____ _____. She _____ one daughter and _____ grandchildren, a _____ and a _____. They are _____ and _____ years old. There is a problem. When we go to their house or eat at a restaurant I try_____ _____ to the two grandchildren. But _____ _____ playing games on their iPhones all _____ _____. All I get are _____-_____ answers. I think this is _____ rude.

I think _____ _____ wrong. I want _____ _____ something about this, but my wife doesn't want me _____ _____ to her daughter _____ son-in-law or to the children _____ _____ . She says that this is the way it is now. Times are changing. _____ _____ we are going to be _____ _____ again with them. I don't want _____ _____ .What should _____ _____ ?

Harry

Discussion

1. What should Harry do?
2. Do you think that the children are rude?
3. "Times are changing." Do you agree?
4. Do you have your I-Phone out when you are talking to people?
5. Do you know people who play games on their I-Phones all the time?

Basic Dictations © 2013 Catherine Sadow and Judy DeFilippo

Teacher's note:
CD track 7
Full text 119
Instuctions
for doing the
dictation:
page 116

Man's Best Friend

Introduction

Are you a dog lover? Many people say that a dog is man's best friend. We treat dogs like members of the family, and they are always happy to see us when we come home. People in many countries of the world love their dogs. Here is some information about Americans and their dogs.

Vocabulary and Pronunciation

1. **cemetery**: a place where you put people who have died
2. **percent**: %
3. **puppy**: a young dog
4. **veterinarian** (vet): an animal doctor

Pair Dictation, Student A - Dictate to each other..

---

1. 40% of U.S. homes _____ _____ _____ _____ .

2. 43% cook _____ _____ for their dogs.

3. _____ _____ _____ give their pets _____ _____

    _____ _____

4. 33% talk to their pets _____ _____ _____ .

5. 84% _____ _____ the dog's " _____" or

    "_____ ."

Discussion 1

1. Do you have a dog?
2. In your country:
    a. do dogs live inside or outside the house?
    b. do dogs ever sleep in the same room or same bed as people?
    c. do people cook special food for their dogs?
    d. do you have animal hospitals and animal cemeteries?

*Teacher's note:
CD track 3
Full text 119
Instuctions
for doing the
dictation:
page 116*

Pair Dictation, Student B - Dictate to each other.

1. _____ _____ _____ _____ have a pet dog.

2. _____ _____ special food _____ _____

    _____.

3. 79% of Americans _____ _____ _____

    Christmas or birthday gifts.

4. _____ _____ _____ _____

    _____ on the phone.

5. _____ call themselves _____ _____ "mother" or

    "father."

Listening

Listen carefully and put a checkmark beside the sentences you hear.

____✓____ 1. Can I have a puppy?

_____ 2. Can I have a dog?

_____ 3. I will do everything.

_____ 4. I can do that.

_____ 5. Can you take the dog out before you go to school?

_____ 6. But I have to be at school by nine o'clock.

_____ 7. Also you have to train the dog.

_____ 8. What kind of dog do you want?

_____ 9. Maybe we can get a cat.

_____ 10. I'll think about it.

Discussion 2

1. Some dogs are trained to help people, such as seeing-eye dogs. Do you know of any other ways dogs help people?

2. Here are some breeds of dogs. What breeds are popular in your country?

German Shepherd	French Poodle	Boston Terrier	Chihuahua
Cocker Spaniel	Pug	Golden Retriever	Shih Tzu

Basic Dictations © 2013 Catherine Sadow and Judy DeFilippo

Let's Talk

Teacher's note: CD track 8 Full text 120 Instuctions for doing the dictation: page 116

Introduction

Many people write to newspapers about their problems and ask for advice.

Vocabulary and Pronunciation

1. **checking your cell phone**: looking to see if there are messages
2. **texting**: sending or answering messages by writing on your phone
3. **teenage**: between the ages of twelve and twenty

Partial Dictation - Listen and fill in the blank spaces.

Dear Friend,

I _____ our family _____ _____ to each other more, but _____ _____ very difficult. We are _____ people, my husband and I and a teenage _____ and a teenage daughter. Everyone in our _____ has a cell phone, and we also have _____ television sets and four computers. At breakfast _____ _____ _____. My children and my husband _____ _____ their breakfast and checking their _____ _____ . At night my _____ goes to his _____ to do his homework and _____ videogames on his _____ . My daughter _____ _____ _____ _____ to do her homework and _____ to her friends on her phone. My husband goes to the living room to _____ news and baseball. I feel very alone. No one in our family talks. What _____ ____ _____ ?

Sad Mother

Discussion

1. What do you think "Sad Mother" can do to make her family talk to each other more?
2. Do you think this is a common problem? Is it a problem for you and your family?
3. Is it a problem only in rich countries?

Am I Too Old?   Asking for Advice

*Teacher's note:
CD track 9
Full text 120
Instructions for doing the dictation: page 116*

Introduction

A young grandmother writes a letter to the newspaper and asks for advice.

Vocabulary

1. **grandma**: a short name for grandmother
2. **retire**: to stop working when you get older
3. **widow**: a woman whose husband has died

Pair Dictation, Student A - Dictate to each other.

Dear _____,

_____ _____ 71 _____ _____ . _____ _____ a widow.

I _____ from my job _____ _____ _____ five years ago. _____

_____ two sons, _____ they live _____ _____

_____ .

   My sons _____ want me _____ _____ . They say _____

_____ too old. _____ _____ don't drive, _____ _____ have to _____

_____ a lot. _____ _____ I do?

                                          Young Grandma

Match the following

___ Her sons think	a. two sons
___ They don't want her	b. she retired
___ She is	c. to drive
___ Five years ago	d. a nurse
___ She doesn't want	e. a widow
___ She was	f. to stay home
___ She has	g. she is too old to drive

Basic Dictations © 2013 Catherine Sadow and Judy DeFilippo

Pair Dictation   **Student B** - Dictate to each other.

_____ Friend,

    I am _____ years old. I am _____ _____ . _____ retired _____

_____ _____ as a nurse _____ _____ _____ . I have _____

_____, but _____ _____ in different cities.

    _____ _____ don't _____ _____ to drive. _____ _____

I am _____ _____ . If I _____ _____ I will _____ _____ stay

home _____ _____ . What should _____ _____ ?

Young Grandma

Dictogloss - Listen once, then write what you remember. With a partner, try to reconstruct the sentence.

1.

2.

3.

Discussion

1. What do you think she should do?
2. What are some of the reasons her sons want her to stop driving?
3. When do you think people should stop driving? Why?

Who is Important?

*Teacher's note:
CD track 10
Full text 121
Instuctions
for doing the
dictation:
page 116*

Introduction

Look at the following questions. It is not necessary to answer all of them, but someone in your class may know one or two names. Guess if you can!

1. Can you name three very rich people in the world?
2. Can you name three people who have won the Nobel Prize?
3. Can you name three Academy Award winners for best actor or actress?

Vocabulary and Pronunciation

1. **dependable**: responsible, trustworthy
2. **talkative**: likes to talk
3. **good sense of humor**: likes to laugh and enjoys a good joke

Partial Dictation - Listen and fill in the blank spaces.

1. Name _____ _____ _____ who _____ you in school or college.

2. Name three friends who have helped you through a _____

   _____.

3. Think of three people you enjoy _____ _____ _____.

4. _____ _____ a few people whom _____ _____.

Discussion

1. "Famous people, like the ones in the introduction, are important, but we quickly forget their names." Why? Are these people important to us personally?

2. "The people who make a difference in your life are not the richest or the most famous. They are simply the ones who care the most." Do you agree or disagree with this statement? Explain.

3. Here are some adjectives that you can use to describe people. Choose the adjectives you would use to describe your _____. (a. mother or father, b. best friend, c. sister or brother) Add more if you think of more.

   caring, fun-loving, a good sense of humor, dependable, smart, talkative

Basic Dictations © 2013 Catherine Sadow and Judy DeFilippo

Using Numbers

Teacher's note:
CD track 11
Full text 121
Instructions for doing the dictation: page 116

Introduction/Vocabulary/Pronunciation

Practice the pronunciation of these numbers with your teacher.

Zero (oh) one two three four five six seven eight nine ten
0   1   2   3   4   5   6   7   8   9   10

STUDENT ID CARD

NAME • NOMBRE • NOM
SARA LINDON

ADDRESS • DIRECCION • ADRESSE
470 Main St

CITY • CIUDAD • VILLE
San Diego

STATE • ESTADO • PROVINCIA • ETAT
California

TELEPHONE • TELEFONO • TELEPHONE
907-245-5163

ZIP CODE • ZONA POSTALE • CODE POSTAL
94087

1. What is her first name?

2. What is her last name?

3. What is her address?

4. What is her zip code?

5. What is her telephone number?

Partial Dictation - Listen and fill in the blank spaces.

1. My telephone number is _____.

2. His address is _____ Washington Street.

3. Her zip code is _____.

4. Her I.D. number is _____.

5. His email address is _____.

Discussion, Part 1

Ask and answer questions about this information.

IDENTIFICATION
Name: Sue Young Kim   **Street:** 742 Evergreen Terrace
City: Boston   **State:** Massachusetts (MA)   **Zip:** 02115
Telephone: 617-223-5690

Discussion, Part 2

Do you know the telephone numbers for:
a. An emergency call   b. A good doctor   c. A good dentist   d. A nearby hospital

More With Numbers

Introduction/Vocabulary/Pronunciation

Teacher's note:
CD track 12
Full text 121
Instuctions
for doing the
dictation:
page 116

Practice pronouncing the following ordinal numbers with your teacher.

1	first	1st	11	eleventh	11th	21	twenty-first	21st
2	second	2nd	12	twelfth	12th	22	twenty-second	22nd
3	third	3rd	13	thirteenth	13th	23	twenty-third	23rd
4	fourth	4th	14	fourteenth	14th	24	twenty-fourth	24th
5	fifth	5th	15	fifteenth	15th	25	twenty-fifth	25th
6	sixth	6th	16	sixteenth	16th	26	twenty-sixth	26th
7	seventh	7th	17	seventeenth	17th	27	twenty-seventh	27th
8	eighth	8th	18	eighteenth	18th	28	twenty-eighth	28th
9	ninth	9th	19	nineteenth	19th	29	twenty-ninth	29th
10	tenth	10th	20	twentieth	20th	30	thirtieth	30th

Pair Dictation, Student A - Dictate to each other.

Example: On Wednesday, September 2nd, there is a full moon.

SEPTEMBER						
SUN	**MON**	**TUES**	**WED**	**THURS**	**FRI**	**SAT**
		1	2 Full Moon	3	4	5 family party 3:00
6	7 Labor Day	8	9 first day of class	10	11	12
13 birthday party	14	15	16	17	18	19
20	21	22	23 birthday party	24	25	26
27	28	29 doctor's appointment	30 Blue Moon			

Pair Dictation, Student B - Dictate to each other.

Example: On Wednesday, September 2nd, there is a full moon.

SEPTEMBER						
SUN	**MON**	**TUES**	**WED**	**THURS**	**FRI**	**SAT**
		1	2 Full Moon	3	4	5
dinner with 6 the Smiths at 5	7 Labor Day	8	9	10	11	baseball 12 game
13	14	dentist 15 2:00	16	17	18	19
20	21	hair 22 4:00	23	24	25	26
27	28	29	birthday 30 3:00 Blue Moon			

Discussion - Work with a partner.

1. Labor Day is the only American holiday in September. It is always the first Monday of the month. In many countries people celebrate this holiday on May first. What does "labor" mean and why is this a holiday? What date is it on this calendar?

2. Labor Day is also the day people say is the end of summer. The actual last day of summer is usually September 21st. It is not a holiday. Do you have an official "end of summer" time in your culture? Or a back-to-school time?

3. Are there any holidays in your country in September? Tell the class, if there are.

4. Does someone in this class or in your family have a birthday in September? Tell the class when it is.

American Money

*Teacher's note:
CD track 13
Full text 122
Instuctions
for doing the
dictation:
page 116*

Introduction/Vocabulary/Pronunciation

It is important to know the names of American coins and bills. Here is some practice!

| a penny | a nickel | a dime | a quarter |
| one cent | five cents | ten cents | twenty-five cents |

| a one-dollar bill | a five-dollar bill | a ten-dollar bill | a twenty-dollar bill |

Practice saying these amounts.

$1.25 $5.05 $25.50 $10.10 $2.35 $7.99

Partial Dictation - Listen and fill in the blank spaces.

1. Jen has two _____ , three dimes, _____ nickel, two quarters, _____
   a five- _____ _____ How much money _____ _____ ?

2. Ben is buying a hat. It's _____ . He has a twenty-dollar _____ .
   How much _____ his change?

3. A shoe store is having _____ sale. Bob _____ _____ two pairs
   of sneakers at $_____ each. How much money _____ _____ ?

4. The _____ members of the Baxter family _____ in a restaurant eating
   dinner. Each dinner is $ _____ . How much is the _____ ?

Discussion

1. Sue has $55. She wants to buy a sweater for $35, a scarf for $12, and a hat for $9.
   Can she buy all three?

2. What can you buy for $.25? $.50? $1.00?

A Little Math • Add and Subtract

Teacher's note:
CD track 14
Full text 122
Instuctions
for doing the
dictation:
page 116

Introduction/Vocabulary/Pronunciation

Practice the pronunciation of these words with your teacher.

1. add $+$

2. subtract $-$

3. circle ◯

4. triangle ◺

5. line ——

6. above, over <u>●</u> the line

7. below, under <u>   </u>● the line

8. lines in a row —— —— ——

9. middle, center (line) —— —— ——

Partial Dictation - Listen and fill in the blank spaces. Then follow the instructions.

1. Draw _____ lines in a row. Write _____ on the first _____ . Write
   _____ on the last line. Add the two numbers together. _____ your
   answer _____ _____ middle line.

2. Draw _____ lines in a row. Write _____ on the _____ line.
   Write _____ on the second _____ . Subtract the smaller number
   _____ the bigger number. _____ your answer on the middle _____ .

3. Draw a circle. Write _____ above the _____ . Write _____

   below the circle. Subtract the _____ number from the

   _____ number. Write _____ answer inside the circle.

4. _____ a triangle. _____ _____ over the triangle. Write _____

   under the triangle. Add the numbers together and write the answer inside the

   _____ .

5. _____ a circle. _____ a triangle under the circle. Put _____ in the

   circle. Put _____ in the triangle. _____ the numbers together. Put your

   answer below the triangle.

Discussion

Describe Figure A to your partner. Then your partner will describe Figure B to you.

FIG. A

100

① **1**

100

FIG. B

Fun With Numbers

Teacher's
note:
CD track 15
Full text 123
Instuctions
for doing the
dictation:
page 116

Introduction/Vocabulary/Pronunciation

Practice the pronunciation of these words with your teacher.

1. multiply   ✕

2. divide   ÷

3. times   ✕   Five <u>times</u> two is ten.

4. circle ◯

5. line   ——

6. (lines) in a row   —— —— ——

7. over, above   ● the line

8. under, below —— the line
     ●

9. triangle ◺

Partial Dictation

- Fill in the blank spaces. Spell all numbers from one to ten. Write numerals for 11 and above.

1. Draw _____ lines in a row. Write _____ on the second _____ .
   Write _____ on the first line. Multiply the _____ _____
   and put the answer _____ _____ _____ line.

2. Draw a circle. Above the _____, write _____. Below the circle, write
   _____. Divide the _____ number by the smaller number. Put the
   answer in the circle.

3. Draw _____ lines _____ _____ _____. Write the number _____ on

the first _____ and the number _____ on the second line. Multiply the

two numbers and put your answer _____ _____ _____ _____ .

Dictogloss - Listen once, then write what you remember. With a partner, try to reconstruct the sentence.

1.

2.

Listening

Listen to the short lecture. Fill in the chart as you listen.

Number	Lucky / Unlucky	East / West
3		East
4	Unlucky	
7	Lucky	
13		

Teacher's note:
CD track 16
Full text 124
Instuctions
for doing the
dictation:
page 116

Trivia Contest!

Introduction

A contest is a game with winners and losers. Trivia is defined as information that is not important but is often fun to know.

Partial Dictation

After you fill in the blank spaces, work together in groups of three – quietly so other groups don't hear your answers – and answer as many questions as you can. Guess if you don't know. Assign one person as secretary to write down your answers. Your teacher will collect your answers. The group with the most correct answers wins!

---

1. _____ _____ _____ do Americans celebrate Valentine's Day?

2. What does _____/_____ stand for?

3. What percent (%) is _____ _____ _____ in a restaurant?

4. _____ _____ _____ a pack of cigarettes?

5. What is the average yearly salary of a _____ _____

   _____ ?

6. How much sleep _____ _____ _____ need each night?

7. _____ _____ _____ do Angelina Jolie and Brad Pitt have?

8. What is the average total time a commuter travels _____ _____

   _____ _____ ?

9. What is _____ _____ _____ temperature in Fahrenheit?

10. _____ _____ do many Americans think is unlucky?

Discussion

With a partner, guess what the answers might be and share them with your class. There are no right or wrong answers.

Example: Her grandmother is old. How old is old?   <u>90</u> (one student)
                                                          <u>80</u> (the other student)

1. She has a lot of children. How many does she have?   _____

2. She works long hours every day. How many hours?   _____

3. She spends too much time on her iPad. How much time?   _____

4. She makes a lot of money. How much per week?   _____

5. She watches too much television every day. How much?   _____

6. She has a long drive to work. How many minutes?   _____

Teacher's note:
CD track 17
Full text 124
Instructions for doing the dictation: page 116

What Time Is It? Part 1

Introduction

Look at the clocks and practice saying the times.

 **1:00**    **7:00**    **12:00**

It's one o'clock.

 **6:00**    **3:00**    **9:00**

Partial Dictation

Listen to the store hours and write in the correct times. A.M. is morning and P.M. is afternoon. Use :00 with numerals (1:00 – 12:00).

1. The Higgins Hospital Visiting Hours are from _____ P.M. to _____ P.M.

2. The South School is open from _____ A.M. to _____ P.M.

3. The car repair shop business hours are _____ A.M. to _____ P.M.

4. The store hours for Bob's Bookstore are

    Sundays _____ to _____.

    Mon. through Sat. _____ to _____.

5. The hours for Terry's Restaurant are

    Lunch: _____ A.M. to _____ P.M.

    Dinner: _____ P.M. to _____ P.M.

6. The North River Medical Center's hours are

    Monday through Friday, _____ A.M. to _____ P.M.

    Weekends, emergencies only, _____ A.M. to _____ P.M.

Photocopyable for classroom use.   Basic Dictations © 2013 Catherine Sadow and Judy DeFilippo

Discussion 1

1. What time do supermarkets usually open in the morning?
   _____ or _____.

2. What time do public schools usually close in the afternoon?
   _____ or _____.

3. Name two places that are open 24 hours a day.
   _____ and _____.

4. What is a good time for you to eat dinner?

5. What is a good time for you to go to bed?

6. What time do you usually get up in the morning?

Discussion 2

With a partner, write in the opening and closing hours of the following places. Then share your answers with the class.

WORLD GYM Hours Mon. – Fri. Sat. – Sun.	FIRST BANK Hours Mon. – Fri. Sat.	PHARMACY Hours Mon. – Sun.

Follow up

Find out the hours of the following places.

1. A supermarket near you

2. A U. S. post office near you

3. A library near you

What Time Is It? Part 2

Teacher's note:
CD track 18
Full text 125
Instuctions
for doing the
dictation:
page 116

Introduction

Practice saying the times. Draw the hands on the clocks.

3:00   3:15   2:30   3:45

9:00   9:15   9:30   9:45

6:00   6:15   6:30   6:45

Partial Dictation

Listen to the times for the Milton bus schedule and write them on the correct line.

MILTON BUS COMPANY

Daily service

Tickets

One way - $ _____

Round trip - $ _____

Milton to Newton		*Newton to Milton*	
Leaves Milton	Arrives Newton	Leaves Newton	Arrives Milton
_____	_____	_____	_____
_____	_____	_____	_____
_____	_____	_____	_____

Discussion 1

Look at the bus schedule and answer these questions.

1. When does the first bus leave Milton and when does it arrive in Newton?

2 How long is the bus trip from Milton to Newton?

3. When does the 11:15 A.M. bus arrive in Newton?

4. How many morning trips are there to Newton?

5. A one-way ticket from Milton to Newton is _____ and round trip is _____.

6. Tell your partner what the schedule is from Newton back to Milton.

7. You arrive in Newton at 8:15 A.M. and spend all day there with a friend. The last bus you can take home leaves at _____.

8. Going to work, your friend's sister always takes the 7:00 bus to Milton. She finishes work at 6:00 P.M. What bus can he take back home to Newton?

Discussion 2

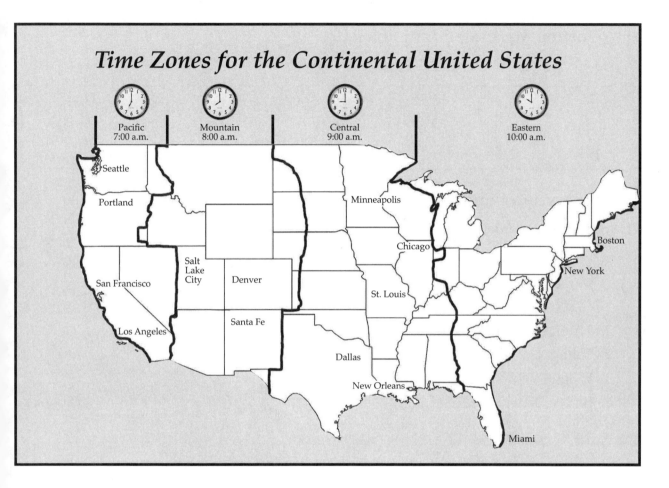

Time Zones for the Continental United States

Pacific
7:00 a.m.

Mountain
8:00 a.m.

Central
9:00 a.m.

Eastern
10:00 a.m.

Seattle

Portland

Minneapolis

Chicago

Boston

Salt
Lake
City

Denver

San Francisco

St. Louis

New York

Los Angeles

Santa Fe

Dallas

New Orleans

Miami

1. You are in Los Angeles, California. The time is 7:00 P.M. What time is it in New York City?

2. What is the time difference between New York and California?

3. It's 10:00 A.M. in Miami, Florida. What time is it in Boston, Massachusetts?

4. You are in Dallas, Texas. It's 11:00 A.M. What time is it in Chicago, Illinois?

5. It's 10:00 P.M. in Denver, Colorado. What time is it in San Francisco?

6. What is the time difference between the city you are in now and the city you came from?

7. Is there more than one time zone in your country?

Teacher's note:
CD track 19
Full text 125
Instuctions for doing the dictation: page 116

The Days of the Week

Introduction/Vocabulary/Pronunciation

Here are the days of the week! Practice saying them.

Sunday	Monday	Tuesday	Wednesday	Thursday	Friday	Saturday
SUN	MON	TUES	WED	THURS	FRI	SAT
S	M	T	W	T or TH	F	S

Vocabulary and Pronunciation

Say these words, and then circle the one word that doesn't belong.

Example: one, ten, (name,) fifteen

1. Monday, Friday, Holiday, Sunday
2. Days, Tuesday, Months, Years
3. Thurs., Sat., Wed., Sunday
4. Today, How long, How many, How much
5. What, When, Wednesday, Why
6. Before, After, Weekend, On

Partial Dictation - Listen and fill in the blank spaces.

1. What days _____ _____ in English class?
2. What day _____ before_____ ?
3. What day _____ after _____ ?
4. What _____ _____ are the weekend days?
5. _____ _____ do most people go to _____ ?
6. How many days _____ in one _____ ?

Discussion

1. How long is a long weekend? What days are usually in a long weekend?
2. T. G. I. F. is a happy phrase. What does it mean?
3. Sunday is a quiet day for many Americans. Why?
4. What are some things to do on Sundays?
5. What do you like to do on weekends?
6. How many days a week do people work in your country?

The Months of the Year

Teacher's note:
CD track 20
Full text 125
Instuctions
for doing the
dictation:
page 116

Introduction

Look at the calendar. With your teacher, practice saying the names of the months.

JANUARY 1st						
Sun	Mon	Tue	Wed	Thu	Fri	Sat
		1	2	3	4	5
6	7	8	9	10	11	12
13	14	15	16	17	18	19
20	21	22	23	24	25	26
27	28	29	30	31		

FEBRUARY 2nd						
Sun	Mon	Tue	Wed	Thu	Fri	Sat
					1	2
3	4	5	6	7	8	9
10	11	12	13	14	15	16
17	18	19	20	21	22	23
24	25	26	27	28		

MARCH 3rd						
Sun	Mon	Tue	Wed	Thu	Fri	Sat
					1	2
3	4	5	6	7	8	9
10	11	12	13	14	15	16
17	18	19	20	21	22	23
24	25	26	27	28	29	30
31						

APRIL 4th						
Sun	Mon	Tue	Wed	Thu	Fri	Sat
	1	2	3	4	5	6
7	8	9	10	11	12	13
14	15	16	17	18	19	20
21	22	23	24	25	26	27
28	29	30				

MAY 5th						
Sun	Mon	Tue	Wed	Thu	Fri	Sat
		1	2	3	4	
5	6	7	8	9	10	11
12	13	14	15	16	17	18
19	20	21	22	23	24	25
26	27	28	29	30	31	

JUNE 6th						
Sun	Mon	Tue	Wed	Thu	Fri	Sat
						1
2	3	4	5	6	7	8
9	10	11	12	13	14	15
16	17	18	19	20	21	22
23	24	25	26	27	28	29
30						

JULY 7th						
Sun	Mon	Tue	Wed	Thu	Fri	Sat
	1	2	3	4	5	6
7	8	9	10	11	12	13
14	15	16	17	18	19	20
21	22	23	24	25	26	27
28	29	30	31			

AUGUST 8th						
Sun	Mon	Tue	Wed	Thu	Fri	Sat
				1	2	3
4	5	6	7	8	9	10
11	12	13	14	15	16	17
18	19	20	21	22	23	24
25	26	27	28	29	30	31

SEPTEMBER 9th						
Sun	Mon	Tue	Wed	Thu	Fri	Sat
1	2	3	4	5	6	7
8	9	10	11	12	13	14
15	16	17	18	19	20	21
22	23	24	25	26	27	28
29	30					

OCTOBER 10th						
Sun	Mon	Tue	Wed	Thu	Fri	Sat
		1	2	3	4	5
6	7	8	9	10	11	12
13	14	15	16	17	18	19
20	21	22	23	24	25	26
27	28	29	30	31		

NOVEMBER 11th						
Sun	Mon	Tue	Wed	Thu	Fri	Sat
					1	2
3	4	5	6	7	8	9
10	11	12	13	14	15	16
17	18	19	20	21	22	23
24	25	26	27	28	29	30

DECEMBER 12th						
Sun	Mon	Tue	Wed	Thu	Fri	Sat
1	2	3	4	5	6	7
8	9	10	11	12	13	14
15	16	17	18	19	20	21
22	23	24	25	26	27	28
29	30	31				

Word Practice

Circle the word that doesn't belong.

Example: three, thirty-three, (two,) three hundred

A. February, June, January, Tuesday
Five, Seven, March, Thirteen
Week, May, Month, Year
School, Teacher, Class, September

B. Yes or No?
_____ 1. January is the first month of the year.
_____ 2. February is before January.
_____ 3. December is the last month of the year.
_____ 4. There are ten months in a year.
_____ 5. August is after July.

 Basic Dictations © 2013 Catherine Sadow and Judy DeFilippo

Partial Dictation 1

Write the date that you hear. Then write the short form next to it.

Example: <u>January 20, 2015</u> or <u>1/20/2015</u>
         month day, year   month/day/year

1. _____ or _____
2. _____ or _____
3. _____ or _____
4. _____ or _____
5. _____ or _____

Partial Dictation 2

Listen and write the words you hear in the blank spaces. Then circle the answer you think is correct. Refer to the calendar on the previous page.

1. Is January _____ _____ _____ ?
   a. Yes, it is.   b. June   c. on Tuesday

2. When is _____ _____ ?
   a. In March   b. No, it isn't.   c. for 2 days

3. _____ _____ _____ does May have?
   a. April   b. 31   c. today

4. When does the _____ _____ _____ ?
   a. In September   b. Yes, it does.   c. Friday night

Discussion

1. My favorite month is _____ because _____.
2. The four months that end in BER are _____.
3. The three months that begin with J are _____.
4. _____ is the shortest month with 28 or 29 days.
5. School vacations in my country are usually in _____.

Teacher's note:
CD track 21
Full text 126
Instuctions for doing the dictation: page 116

The Four Seasons

Introduction and Vocabulary

Many parts of the United States have four very different seasons. Talk about the seasons with your class.

Winter Dec. to March	Spring March to June	Summer June to September	Fall or Autumn September to December

Dictogloss - Listen once, then write what you remember. With a partner, try to reconstruct the sentence.

1. _____

2. _____

3. _____

4. _____

Discussion

1. What season is it if you're _____?
   a. wearing shorts and a T shirt
   b. wearing a big coat, gloves, and boots
   c. wearing a raincoat and carrying an umbrella
   d. going to a football game in jeans and a sweater
2. Do you have four seasons in your country? Explain.
3. There are parts of the United States that don't have four seasons. Can you name any U.S. cities that do not have snow?
4. It's _____ in New York. What season is it?
   a. February   b. May   c. October   d. August

Basic Dictations © 2013 Catherine Sadow and Judy DeFilippo

Teacher's note:
CD track 22
Full text 126
Instuctions
for doing the
dictation:
page 116

What's the Weather? The Temperature?

Introduction/Vocabulary/Pronunciation

Part 1 What's the weather today? It's _____.

sunny   cloudy   rainy   snowy   partly sunny   windy

Part 2 In the United States we use the Fahrenheit scale. With a partner, practice using it with the weather report for New York, Miami, Chicago, Los Angeles, and Seattle.

Student A: What's the weather today in <u>New York</u>?
Student B: It's <u>cold and snowy</u>. It's <u>23</u> degrees.

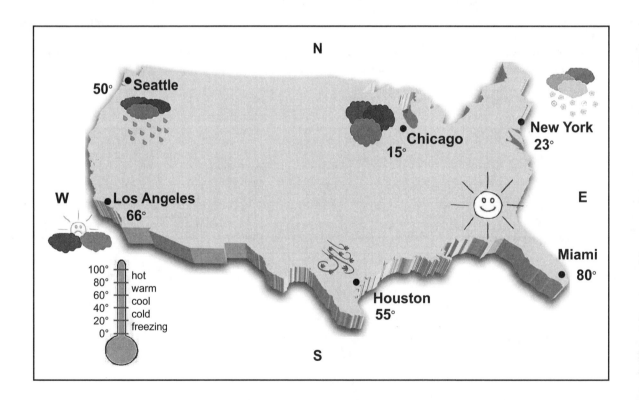

Part 3 Convert from one scale to the other.

For example: **A.** If it's 25 degrees Celsius, what is it in Fahrenheit?
B. It's 77 degrees Fahrenheit.

Fahrenheit	Celsius
-4	-20
5	-15
14	-10
23	-5
32	0
41	5
50	10
59	15
68	20
77	25
86	30
95	35

Converting Fahrenheit to Celsius

1. Subtract 32 from the F temperature
2. Multiply by 5/9

Example: 50 F -32=18
18 X 5/9 = 10

Partial Dictation

Listen and write the information you hear in the correct box. The first one is done for you.

City	Weather	Temperatures
New York	*cold, snowy*	*20s*
Chicago		
Miami		
Houston		
Los Angeles		
Seattle		

Discussion

1. Talk about the city you are in. What is the weather like there today?

2. Does the area you live in now have extreme weather conditions?
   a. big snowstorms   b. floods   c. earthquakes   d. tornadoes

3. In your home country do you have extreme conditions?

4. Do schools close in bad weather? How do you know when school is canceled?

Teacher's note: CD track 23 Full text 126 Instuctions for doing the . dictation: page 116

United States Holidays and Special Days

Introduction

The United States has many holidays and special days. Some are national holidays, such as Independence Day and Memorial Day; some are religious holidays, such as Christmas and Easter; and some are special days.

Vocabulary and Pronunciation

January
New Year's Day (1)

Martin Luther King's
Birthday (15)

February
Lincoln's Birthday (12)

Valentine's Day (14)

Washington's Birthday (22)

March
St. Patrick's Day (17)

1st Day of Spring (21)

April
Good Friday

Easter

Passover

May
Mother's Day

Memorial Day (30)

June
Flag Day (14)

Father's Day

1st Day of Summer (21)

July
Independence Day (4)

August

September
Labor Day (1st Monday)

Rosh Hashanah

1st Day of Fall (21)

October
Columbus Day (12)

Halloween (31)

November
Veterans' Day (11)

Thanksgiving
(4th Thursday)

December
Hanukkah

1st Day of Winter (21)

Christmas (25)

Partial Dictation - Listen and fill in the blank spaces.

1. Name the _____ famous American presidents _____ February birthdays.

2. Name _____ _____ when the U.S. celebrates _____ _____.

3. Are there any _____ _____ _____ ?

4. What two holidays _____ _____ _____ ?

5. What special _____ _____ _____ lovers?

6. What two holidays do _____ _____ ?

Discussion

1. What holidays are religious holidays? national holidays?

2. What food do people eat for Thanksgiving?

3. On what days do we remember people in the military?

4. Labor Day is to celebrate ordinary workers. When is it in your country?

Basic Dictations © 2013 Catherine Sadow and Judy DeFilippo

Teacher's
note:
CD track 24
Full text 127
Instructions
for doing the
dictation:
page 116

Let's Go Shopping!

Introduction/Vocabulary/Pronunciation

Repeat after your teacher.

blouse	*shirt*	*hat*	*pants*	*backpack*
shoes	*coat*	*socks*	*belt*	*jacket*
dress	*tie*	*boots*	*scarf*	*shorts*
gloves	*stockings*	*sweater*	*bra*	*skirt*

Colors

red   white   blue   yellow   purple   green   black   navy blue   maroon
orange   gray   silver   gold   aqua   brown   beige   pink

Sizes

Extra small (XS)   Small (S)   Medium (M)   Large (L)   Extra large (XL)

Phrases

A pair of jeans / socks / shoes / boots   short / long sleeves   a short skirt   a green jacket

Pair Dictation, Student A - Dictate to each other.

How much is this coat on sale?

_____ _____.

What is the regular price of the coat?

_____ _____. _____ _____ _____!

That's a good price!

_____ , _____ _____ _____ _____ _____ _____

_____ _____ .

That's great. I'll take it.

_____ _____ _____?

Cash.

     Basic Dictations © 2013 Catherine Sadow and Judy DeFilippo

Pair Dictation, Student B - Dictate to each other.

_____ _____ ____ ____ _____ _____ _____?

It's $20.00

_____ ____ _____ _____ _____ ___ ____

_____?

It's $30.00. You save $10.00!

_____ ____ _____ _____!

Yes, and today you can buy it for $15.00.

_____ _____. _____ _____ _____.

Cash or charge?

_____.

Practice

With a partner, practice the dialogue with the clothes pictured here. For the word "coat," substitute "sweater," "tie," "Tee shirt," "jacket," and "shirt."

SALE: $18.00   SALE: $8.00   SALE: $5.00   SALE: $40.00   SALE: $12.00
Regular: $20.00   Regular: $10.00   Regular: $7.00   Regular: $45.00   Regular: $15.00

Discussion

1. Many American men wear a white shirt and tie to work. What occasions do men in your country wear a suit?
2. Name two or three articles of clothing that you wear in cold weather.
3. Name two or three articles of clothing you wear in warm weather.
4. Your mother's birthday is soon. What can you buy her?
5. You are in a store. You don't plan to buy anything. You are just looking. When the salesperson asks, "Can I help you?", what do you say?

Second-Hand Clothing Stores

Teacher's note:
CD track 25
Full text 127
Instuctions
for doing the
dictation:
page 116

Introduction

There are many places where you can buy second-hand or used clothes at a great savings. Most churches have small thrift shops and in many states you can find places run by the Salvation Army and Goodwill Industries. There are, of course, large discount stores that sell new clothing such, as Costco and Walmart.

Vocabulary and Pronunciation

1. **second-hand clothing**: clothing that someone else used
2. **department store**: a large store like Macy's and Sears

Partial Dictation - Listen and fill in the blank spaces.

This is Sam. He _____ from San Francisco. He is _____ classmate. He goes shopping at _____ Goodwill Store. He can save _____ because the clothes there _____ second hand. That means his clothes _____ used. At the Goodwill _____ he can buy a warm winter jacket _____ $25.00. That's _____ good price. The _____ is clean and comfortable. Today _____ is wearing black _____ from the Salvation Army Store. They _____ new, not used! The price tag is still on them. The price _____ only $15.00!

Discussion

1. Can you name discount clothing stores? Or outlets? Are they near your neighborhood?
2. Why do people shop at thrift stores?
3. Most stores have a return policy. What is that?
4. What is a sales slip? Why is it important to keep it?
5. You like a sweater but you are looking for a blue one. The only ones you see on the counter are green and red. What do you say to the sales person?
6. What does "shop till you drop" mean? What is a shopaholic?
7. What is a bargain hunter?

*Teacher's note:
CD track 26
Full text 127
Instuctions
for doing the
dictation:
page 116*

Household Items

Introduction/Vocabulary/Pronunciation

Part A. Practice saying the words for furnishings with your teacher.

tables   beds   sofa   chair   washer

refrigerator   stove   bookcase   mirror   towel

rugs   pots and pans   lamp   dishes   pillows

Part B. Name things that belong in these rooms.

Living Room   *Bathroom*   *Kitchen*   *Bedroom*

Prediction Dictation

Fill in each blank. When you are finished, you will listen and do the dictation on the next page. Then compare your responses.

Chen

Hi. My name _____ Chen. I am 23 years _____ . I am from Beijing, China, and I _____ with my family in Chinatown _____ San Francisco. Our _____ building has four floors. Our apartment is on the second _____ . It's comfortable. There _____ a kitchen, a _____ room, two bedrooms, and _____ bathroom. I share a _____ with my two brothers.   My brothers and I _____ students. My parents work _____ a small grocery _____ nearby. I love my _____ a lot. We are happy here _____ _____ United States.

Discussion 1

1. Where in San Francisco does Chen live?
2. How many floors does his apartment building have?
3. How many rooms does his apartment have?
4. How many brothers does Chen have?
5. Where do his parents work?
6. Do Chen and his brothers work?
7. Are they happy here in the United States?

Discussion 2

1. Tell your partner about your apartment, house, or other living arrangements.
2. What furniture do you have? What do you still need?
3. How many people live with you? Are they family? Friends?
4. What do you like about your place?
5. What don't you like about it?

 Basic Dictations © 2013 Catherine Sadow and Judy DeFilippo

Listening Dictation - Listen and fill in the blank spaces.

Chen

Hi. my name _____ Chen. I am 23 years _____ . I am from Beijing, China,

and I _____ with my family in Chinatown _____ San Francisco. Our

_____ building has four floors. Our apartment is on the second

_____ . It's comfortable. There _____ a kitchen, a _____

room, two bedrooms and _____ bathroom. I share a _____ with

my two brothers. My brothers and I _____ students. My parents work _____

a small grocery _____ nearby. I love my _____ a lot. We are

happy here _____ _____ United States.

Used Furnishings

Teacher's note:
CD track 27
Full text 128
Instuctions for doing the dictation: page 116

Introduction

New furnishings are expensive. Many people buy used or second-hand furniture and appliances. You can buy them from ads in the newspaper, through online websites, at yard sales, or from friends.

Vocabulary, Part 1

Abbreviations you will find in ads:

Excel. = excellent   **Cond.** = condition   **Gen. Elec.** = General Electric   " = inches

Vocabulary, Part 2

1. **Sofa bed**, 72" long, double bed size, like new, brown, $75.00, clean

2. **Dryer**, excel. cond., Gen. Elec. white, $85,

3. **Flat screen TV**, 32" screen, $425.00 like new. Sony.

4. **Sewing machine**, Singer Model 327, 1990. OK cond. Asking $60.

Pair Dictation, Student A - Dictate to each other.

I'm calling about your sewing machine.

_____. _____ _____ _____ _____ _____.

What condition is it in?

_____ , _____ _____ _____. _____ ____ _____.

How much would it cost to fix it ?

_____ _____ _____. _____ _____ _____.

Thank you.

Basic Dictations © 2013 Catherine Sadow and Judy DeFilippo

Pair Dictation, Student B - Dictate to each other.

_____ _____ _____ _____ _____ _____.

Yes. It's a Singer Model 327.

_____ _____ _____ _____ _____ ?

Well, it needs repair. It's a 1990.

_____ _____ _____ ____ _____ _____ _____ _____ ?

Probably about $50. I'm not sure.

_____ _____.

Discussion

1. Do you think the caller will buy the sewing machine? Why not?

2. What other information should you ask about?

Practice

Try the dialogues with the TV, the dryer, and the sofa bed with a partner. Use your own ideas!

Basic Dictations © 2013 Catherine Sadow and Judy DeFilippo

Looking for an Apartment

Teacher's note:
CD track 28
Full text 128
Instuctions for doing the dictation: page 116

Introduction/Vocabulary/Pronunciation

When you are looking for an apartment, you look on line or in a newspaper. There are some abbreviations you need to know when you are looking.

Most ads you read will have these abbreviations.

apt. - apartment	**incl**.- including	**renov**. - renovated
avail. - available	**kit**. - kitchen	**std**. - studio
bdrm. - bedroom (or: **br**)	**lge**. - large	**util**. - utilities
gar. **pkg**. - garage parking	**laund**. - laundry	
H&HW - heat and hot water	**mo**. - month	

Practice

Describe these apartments.

FOR RENT IN BOSTON

1. $1600 mo. 2bdrm. – 2 bath – HT/HW incl – gar. Pkg – eat-in kit. AVAIL. May 1

2. $1325/1 br – 1 bath – furn. – in-unit laund. – pet OK, free H/hot water – pkg

Dictogloss - Listen once, then write what you remember. With a partner, try to reconstruct the sentence.

1. _____ .

2. _____ .

3. _____ .

4. _____ .

Discussion

Here are some questions to ask when looking for an apartment. With a partner, decide which questions are the most important. Then think of questions you think are important. Use your dictionaries for new vocabulary. Do a "telephone role play" with a partner. Call, ask, and respond.

1. Is the apartment building quiet?
2. Is the apartment clean?
3. Is the refrigerator included? Heat and utilities?
4. Is there a laundry area? Fire escape? Elevator?
5. Do we sign a lease? For how long?
6. Is there a security deposit? How much?
7. Your questions

Sending Money Home by Western Union

Teacher's note:
CD track 29
Full text 128
Instuctions
for doing the
dictation:
page 116

Introduction

Mr. and Mrs. Gonzales shop at the "Stop and Shop" supermarket every Friday. Once a month they go to the information counter and send money to Mr. Gonzales' mother in Bogota, Colombia. They send it through Western Union, a large company that has been sending money from city to city, state to state, and country to country for over 100 years. Mr. Gonzales' mother will get the money the next day.

Vocabulary and Pronunciation

1. **currency**: money
2. **currency exchange**: changing one country's money to another country's money
3. **fee**: money you pay for help or assistance
4. **transfer fee**: extra money you pay for moving money from one place to another place

Partial Dictation - Listen and fill in the blank spaces.

Mr. and Mrs. Gonzales _____ _____ _____ information counter at the supermarket. They _____ the clerk that they _____ _____ send money using Western Union. They give the clerk $ _____ and a fee for "Next Day" service. Mr. Gonzales _____ _____ _____ his name and address and his mother's _____ . Then he gives the clerk the _____ of a Western Union store or office _____ _____ _____ . He also _____ a 10-digit money transfer control number (MTCN). After he has done this, _____ _____ _____ _____ in Bogota and tells her the number. Next _____ his mother goes to the store with a Western Union in it. She _____ the clerk her ID and tells him the 10-digit number. He _____ _____ _____ _____ in cash.

Basic Dictations © 2013 Catherine Sadow and Judy DeFilippo

Listening

Listen carefully and answer the following questions. Take notes while you listen if it helps you.

1. Who is making the telephone call?

2. Who is he calling?

3. What does he want?

4. Why?

5. What will the person he is calling do?

6. How will she do it?

7. At the end, what does he say he will do?

Discussion

1. Have you ever heard of Western Union?

2. Have you ever used Western Union?

3. We have many other ways to send money. Why do you think anyone uses Western Union?

4. With a partner, fill in the form on the next page.

   The son's name is Charles Black. He lives at 123 South Street in Detroit, Michigan 34520 (MI). His telephone number is 231-566-0289.

   His mother's name is Wanda Black. She lives at 67 North Street in Boston, Massachusetts (MA). 02310 Her telephone number is 617-234-1234.
   Her e-mail is blackwa15@yahoo.com.

MONEY TRANSFER
Send Transferecia de Dinero - Enviar
WESTERN UNION

 **Gold Card WESTERN UNION**
Name:
6475 79012

Have a Gold Card?
You don't need a form!
Just speak to the Agent.
¿Tiene una Tarjeta Dorada?
Sólo vaya donde el agente.

❶ Transaction Information

Send Amount (Dollars)¹ **$**
Cantidad a Enviar (Dolares)
Destination: State/Country
Destino: Estado/Pais

◯ **Money in Minutes** / Dinero en Minutos

◯ **Next Day (where available)** / Dinero Día Siguiente

◯ **To a Mobile Phone (where available)⁴**
A Teléfono Celular (donde este disponible)
Number with Country Code

◯ **Giro Palsano** **Giro Telegráfico** **¿Con aviso a domicillo?**
With notification?

◯ **Home Delivery: Prepaid Card (USA only)2**

◯ **To Bank Account (where available)3**

❷ Transaction Information

Your First Name	**Middle Initial**
Su Nombre	Inicial del segundo nombre
Last Name	
Apellido	
Street (Apt #)	
Dirección (# de Apto)	

City	**State**	**Zip**
Ciudad	Estado	Código Postal

Phone	
Teléfono	
Email	

Mobile Phone*	
Teléfono Celular*	

* By completing, you authorize us to text you special offers/ messages; you may revoke this authorization at any time. Standard message and data rates may apply. Reply STOP to stop. Reply HELP for help. / * Si completa, usted nos autoríza a enviarte mesajes de texto con ofertas especiales y otro tipo de menajes; usted pueda revocar esta autorizacion en cualquier momento. Tarifas estándares de mensajes y datos se pueden aplicar. Para bloquear mensajes conteste STOP. Conteste HELP para obtener ayuda.

❸ Transaction Information

Write the name of the receiver exactly as it appears on their identification. Escribe el nombre del beneficiario.

Receiver's First Name
Nombre del Beneficiario
Last name(s)
Apellido (Paterno, Materno)

Only for Home Delivery or Giro Telegráfico con Aviso:

Business Name (if applicable)	
Nombre comercial (si aplica)	
Address (Apt #/Suite #)	
Dirección (Apto #/oficina #)	
City	
Ciudad	
State	**Zip**
Estado	Código Postal
Phone and/or Email	

Only for sending to a Bank Account

Bank Name
Nombre de Banco
Routing / Swift / Bank Identifier Code
Número de Enrutamiento
Account Number / IBAN
Número de Cuenta
Other Information
Información Adicional

If sending less than $1,000 to a Receiver in the U.S. that does not have identification. You may provide a test question and answer.

Test Question (limit 4 words)
Pregunta de Prueba (un máximo de cuarto palabras)
Answer
Respuesta

❹ Your Signature / Su firma

 X

Certain terms and conditions governing this transaction and the sevices you have selected are set forth on the attached pages. By signing this receipt, you are agreeing to those terms and conditions.
1,2,3,4 All numbered notes are on the bottom of Page 1.
1,2,3,4 Todas las notas numeradas están en la parte inferior de la página 1.

AGENT USE ONLY / SOLO PARA USO DEL AGENTE

Money Transfer Control No. No. de Control de Envio de Dinero (MTCN)	**Amount** Cantidad	**Transfer Fee** Cargo por el Enviro	**Other fees** Otros Cargos	**Tax** Impuestos	**Total Collected** Cantidad Total	**Exchange Rate** Tipo de Cambio	**Amount to be Paid** Cantidad a pager
☐☐☐☐☐☐☐☐☐☐☐☐☐	$	$	$	$	$	$	$

Agent Copy / Copia del Agente • page 2 | Página 2 | DFMUIFDB (1/12) | AGENT SIGNATURE | DATE

Teacher's note:
CD track 30
Full text 129
Instuctions
for doing the
dictation:
page 116

United States Postal Service (USPS)

Introduction

CD track 30
Full text 129

More and more people are using e-mail and paying bills on the Internet. Do we still need someone to bring us our mail? Do we still need a post office?

Vocabulary and Pronunciation

1. **mail carrier**: the man or woman who brings the mail to you
2. **priority mail**: mail that will get there quicker
3. **package**: a box or bag with something in it
4. **registered mail**: Someone must sign for it when it is delivered.
5. **insured**: If it is lost, you will receive money.

Pair Dictation, Student A - Dictate to each other.

1. _____ _____ _____ has a post office.

2. In small towns _____ _____ _____ _____ _____ at the

   post office.

3. _____ _____ _____ our mail carrier brings mail to us.

4. Free delivery of mail _____ _____ _____ _____ _____

   _____ .

5. _____ _____ _____ it began in 1896.

To Register

REG. FEE $3.50	AUG. 14 2026
POSTAGE $ .40	

FROM
LISA ZHANG
26 TOWER STREET
AUSTIN, TX   ZIP CODE 78755

TO
LEE CHIN
P.O. Box 552
SAN DIEGO, CA   ZIP CODE 92128

Pair Dictation, Student B - Dictate to each other.

1. Almost every town _____ ____ _____ _____ .

2. _____ _____ _____ we often get our mail _____

   _____ _____ _____ .

3. In our town _____ _____ _____ _____

   _____ _____ _____ .

4. _____ _____ _____ _____ began in 1836 in

   the cities.

5. In the countryside _____ _____ _____ _____ .

Discussion

What do you do when you go to the post office?

_____ 1. Change your address.

_____ 2. Buy stamps. (a book, a sheet, or a roll)

_____ 3. Mail a package. (air mail, priority, overnight , book rate)

_____ 4. Buy a postal money order.

_____ 5. Register mail.

_____ 6. Insure a package.

_____ 7. Ask the post office to hold your mail.

_____ 8. _____

_____ 9. _____

_____ 10. _____

Listening

Listen to the conversation, and put a checkmark beside the sentences you hear. Check your answers with your partner.

_____ 1. What can I do for you today?

_____ 2. What do you mean?

_____ 3. We can send it Priority Mail.

_____ 4. Where is it going to?

_____ 5. That will be $99.00.

_____ 6. It's a coffee pot.

_____ 7. That will be $14.72.

_____ 8. Do you need any stamps?

_____ 9. Please give me a book of stamps.

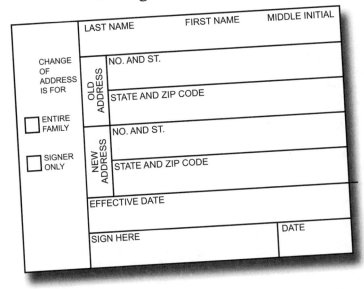

Change of Address

		LAST NAME	FIRST NAME	MIDDLE INITIAL
CHANGE OF ADDRESS IS FOR	OLD ADDRESS	NO. AND ST.		
		STATE AND ZIP CODE		
☐ ENTIRE FAMILY	NEW ADDRESS	NO. AND ST.		
☐ SIGNER ONLY		STATE AND ZIP CODE		
	EFFECTIVE DATE			
	SIGN HERE		DATE	

Public Schools in the United States

Teacher's note:
CD track 31
Full text 130
Instructions
for doing the
dictation:
page 116

Introduction

Public schools in the United States are free for students ages 5 to 18. Some high schools will accept new students who are 19 or 20.

Vocabulary and Pronunciation

1. **pass**: to succeed at a course or test
2. **fail**: do not succeed
3. **grade**: a class level
4. **grade**: an academic mark
5. **average**: the number you find by adding all items in a group and dividing the total by the number of items

Level	Age
Kindergarten	5
Elementary School	
Grades 1 to 5	6 – 10
Middle School	
Grades 6 to 9	11 – 14
High School	
Grades 10 to 12	15 – 18

Letter grades	Number equivalent	Meaning
A	90 – 100	Excellent
B	80 – 89	Good
C	70 – 79	Average
D	60 – 69	Poor
F	0 – 59	Failing

Partial Dictation 1

Listen and write the information you hear in the box.

	Age	Grade	School
John			
Sara			
Ben			
Jenny			

Partial Dictation 2

Listen only once and write the word you hear in the blank space. Refer to the chart in Dictation 1. Circle the correct answer. Then talk about your answers with the class.

1. What grade _____ _____ _____?
   a. Yes, he is.   b. The 6th grade.   c. North Middle School.

2. Is Sara _____ _____ _____?
   a. No, she's seven.   b. Yes, she is.   c. At the High school.

3. How many children are in the _____ _____?
   a. one   b. four   c. two

Basic Dictations © 2013 Catherine Sadow and Judy DeFilippo

Discussion 1

1. Tell your partner about John, Sara, Ben, and Jenny: their ages, grades and schools.
2. Here is Ben's report card from the North Middle School. Refer to the chart at the top of the previous page to see what the letter grades mean. Is he a good student?

REPORT CARD	
ENGLISH	C
MATH	B
HISTORY	A
SCIENCE	B
PHYS ED	B
SPANISH	B

1. What does the grade of _____ mean?
   a. A b. B   c. C
2. What is the number equivalent of _____?
   a. A   b. B   c. C
3. What does average mean?
4. What does failing mean? Is Ben passing all of his courses?

Discussion 2

Part A All four children take the bus to school. Here are their schedules. The Jones family lives at 66 Karr Street.

SCHOOL BUS SCHEDULES
Pick up and drop off at Karr Street

	Pick up	Drop off	
Center School	8:15 AM	2:45 PM	(John & Sara)
North School	7:45 AM	2:15 PM	(Ben)
West School	7:15 AM	1:30 PM	(Jenny)

Part B Talk about the schedule and ask each other questions about the bus schedules. It is not necessary to write the questions.

Example: What time does the bus pick up Ben in the morning?

1.

2.

3.

4.

In the Library

Teacher's note:
CD track 32
Full text 130
Instuctions
for doing the
dictation:
page 116

Introduction

A library card is easy to get, and with it you can borrow books, magazines, CDs, and DVDs for free. Libraries offer many services and events. Many people use the computers, watch films, view art exhibits, spend time in the children's library with their kids, and join book clubs. What other services does your local library have?

Vocabulary and Pronunciation

1. **Kindle**: an electronic book reader (Kindle Fire is a reader and a tablet computer)
2. **DVD**: digital video disc
3. **utility bill**: a bill for your electricity, gas, heating oil, water
4. **ID**: identification

Dictogloss - Listen once, then write what you remember. With a partner, try to reconstruct the sentence.

1. _____

2. _____

3. _____

Listening

Listen to the conversation and put a check mark beside the items that tell you what you need to get a library card. Check your answers with a partner.

_____ two pieces of identification   _____ a driver's license

_____ a Kindle   _____ a library card

_____ a utility bill with your name/address   _____ a student photo ID

Discussion

With a partner talk about the services you know about at your school or town library. Here are a few suggestions.

"Does your library have _____?"   *"No, but it has _____."*

___ children's programs   ___writers coming to talk about their books

___ copy machines   ___ daily newspapers   ___ games for children

___ art exhibits   ___ book clubs   ___ poetry readings   ___ teen movies

Basic Dictations © 2013 Catherine Sadow and Judy DeFilippo

Teacher's note:
CD track 33
Full text 131
Instuctions
for doing the
dictation:
page 116

Keep America Beautiful

Introduction

We need to keep our countries free of litter. Some items that we throw away on the ground can remain in the environment for thousands of years.

Vocabulary and Pronunciation

1. **candy wrapper**: paper covering candy or chocolate
2. **cigarette butt**: the end of a smoked cigarette
3. **environment**: the air, water, and land in which we live
4. **litter**: paper, containers, etc. that people throw on the ground
5. **pollution**: things that make air, water, etc. very dirty
6. **recycle**: put used things through a process so they can be used again
7. **styrofoam cups**: cups that keep coffee or tea hot
8. **trillion**: 1,000,000,000,000

Partial Dictation

- Listen and fill in the blank spaces.

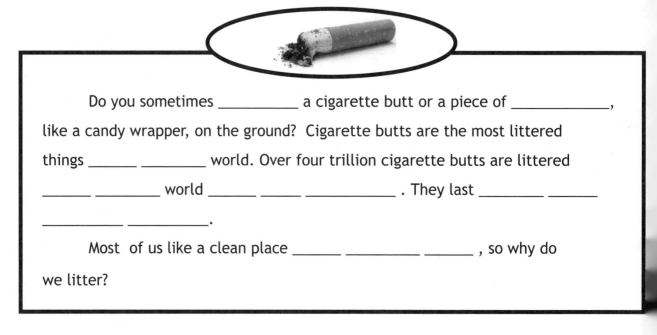

Do you sometimes _____ a cigarette butt or a piece of _____,
like a candy wrapper, on the ground? Cigarette butts are the most littered
things _____ _____ world. Over four trillion cigarette butts are littered
_____ _____ world _____ _____ _____ . They last _____ _____
_____ _____.

Most of us like a clean place _____ _____ _____ , so why do
we litter?

Dictogloss - Listen once, then write what you remember. With a partner, try to reconstruct the sentence.

1.

2.

Listening

Listen to the short lecture, and put a check beside any of the items you hear.

_____ 1. books   _____ 2. bottles

_____ 3. candy wrappers   _____ 4. cigarette butts

_____ 5. fish   _____ 6. motorcycles

_____ 7. newspapers   _____ 8. old cars

_____ 9. plastic containers   _____ 10. soda cans

_____11. styrofoam containers   _____ 12. telephones

_____13. tires   _____ 14. umbrellas

Discussion

1. Do you recycle some things? What do you recycle?
2. Why do some people litter?

     Basic Dictations © 2013 Catherine Sadow and Judy DeFilippo

Teacher's note:
CD track 34
Full text 131
Instuctions
for doing the
dictation:
page 116

Fruit Salad

Introduction

There is going to be a class party. Every student is going to bring something.

Vocabulary and Pronunciation

1. **apples**

2. **bananas**

3. **pears**

4. **grapes**

5. **strawberries**

6. **fruit salad**: a large salad with many different fruits in it
7. **on sale**: the price is lowered
8. **soft drinks**: drinks and juices that are not alcoholic
9. **supermarket**: a large store where you can buy all kinds of food
10. **delicious**: very nice taste

Partial Dictation - Listen and fill in the blank spaces.

The class _____ _____ _____ have a party. Some students _____

_____ cookies. Some students _____ bringing soft drinks.

The teacher _____ _____ coffee and _____. One student

_____ _____ a _____ _____. She is putting

strawberries, _____, pears, _____ _____ in _____

_____ _____ . _____ _____ _____ delicious.

Discussion

1. Do you have class parties?
2. Do you bring something to the class party? What do you bring?
3. Can you cook? What are some of the things you make?
4. What other fruit can you put in a fruit salad?

Listening

Listen to the conversation between a man and a woman and then answer the following questions.

1. Why is the woman making a fruit salad?

2. What is she putting in the fruit salad?

3. What is "on sale" at the supermarket?

Discussion

1. When you go to the supermarket are you confused by the differences between ounces (oz) and pounds (lb) instead of grams and kilograms?

2. Almost the whole world uses grams and kilograms. Why do you think the United States doesn't change to grams and kilograms?

3. In the United States, we usually sell fruit by the pound. $1.99/lb. means that a pound of peaches costs $1.99. If you need about 14 grams of grapes for your fruit salad, how many pounds would you buy?

4. If you need two pounds of fish for dinner tonight, how many kilos of fish should you buy?

1 oz.		28.350 grams
16 oz.	1 lb.	435.59 grams or .4536 kilograms

A Supermarket List

Teacher's
note:
CD track 35
Full text 132
Instuctions
for doing the
dictation:
page 116

CD track 35
Full text 132

Introduction

Some people love to go to the supermarket. Some people hate to go. Do you enjoy shopping in a big supermarket?

Vocabulary and Pronunciation

1. **coupon**: paper from the newspaper or computer that lets you buy something at a lower price
2. **diapers**: worn by babies who are too young to go to the bathroom
3. **list**: a set of words written one below the other
4. **on sale**: it costs less
5. **pasta**: an Italian word for noodles like spaghetti, linguine, lasagnea

Partial Dictation - Listen and fill in the blank spaces.

Mrs. Smith is _____ _____ with their _____ _____ to go to the supermarket. She _____ Mr. Smith a list of things _____ _____. She tells him, "_____ are the important things. Please _____ _____ the diapers. We _____ _____ three _____ _____. We also _____ toilet paper. We have only one roll left. We need _____ and I need _____ sauce. _____ _____ everything on the list."

She also gives him her supermarket card and _____ coupons so he can _____ a lot of things _____ _____. Mr. Smith _____ the list and asks, "Is there anything else _____ _____?" Mrs. Smith says, "I'll _____ _____ on your cell phone if I think of something."

Listening

Listen to the conversation between Mrs. Smith and her husband. While listening, complete the list below, filling in the blank spaces with the numbers, amounts, items, and prices.

	Number	Amount	Item	Price
a.	_____	boxes	diapers	_____
b.	_____	cans	tuna _____	_____
c.	3	_____	_____ sauce	$1.00
d.	1	can	_____	$3.49
e.	_____	rolls	toilet _____	_____
f.	_____	_____	_____ towels	_____
g.	_____	_____	cereal	_____
h.	1.5	lbs. (pounds)	_____ grapes	_____

Circle the correct answer.

Mr. Smith spent about $30.00 $40.00 $50.00 $60.00

Discussion

Part 1 With a partner, discuss the following questions.

1. Do you usually make a list before you go to the supermarket? What happens if you don't have a list with you?

2. Do you sometimes buy things that are not on your list?

3. Do you use coupons from the newspaper or a supermarket card to save money?

Part 2 With a partner, discuss what you might need to buy for the next couple of days. Then, make a shopping list.

1. What food will you need?

2. What other things will you need to buy? Can you get them at the supermarket? If not, where will you try to buy them?

Nothing to Eat!

Teacher's note:
CD track 36
Full text 133
Instuctions
for doing the
dictation:
page 116

Introduction

Lots of people are on diets. Some join diet clubs; others lose weight by themselves by eating salads and cutting down on sweets. Here is a dictation about a boy who IS NOT on a diet. He is writing a letter to you and he needs your advice!

Vocabulary and Pronunciation

1. **starving**: very hungry
2. **on a diet**: trying to lose weight
3. **eat out**: eat in a restaurant
4. **empty**: nothing inside

Partial Dictation - Listen and fill in the blank spaces.

Dear Friend,

Help! There is nothing _____ _____ _____ in my house. Our refrigerator _____ _____. Why? Because my mother, my sister, _____ _____ _____ are all on diets. I AM NOT on a diet, and I _____ _____! I like steak and hamburgers, _____, and _____. I want an ice cream or _____ _____ when I come home _____ _____. My mother is eating only _____ and _____. My sister _____ _____ lots of vegetables and fruits. My grandmother is eating _____ _____ chicken. We never _____ _____. I am going crazy! What _____ _____ _____?

Starving Steven, 17

Discussion

1. Who is on a diet?
2. What food does Steven like?
3. What is his _____ eating?   a. mother   b. sister   c. grandmother
4. What is your advice for Steven?
   a. go on a diet, too   b. eat out every night
   c. eat diet meals at home and other food outside   d. other: do you have a better idea?
5. Do you know the names of famous diet organizations?

Basic Dictations © 2013 Catherine Sadow and Judy DeFilippo

Teacher's note: CD track 37 Full text 133 Instuctions for doing the dictation: page 116

Eat Right!

Meat Group

Introduction

What are your favorite foods? Do you eat fruits and vegetables every day? What other foods do you eat every day? Here is a chart to show important foods you need in your daily diet.

Vegetable Group

Vitamins, Minerals, Carbohydrates

Fruit Group

Protein, Fats, Vitamins

Vitamins, Minerals, Carbohydrates

Vocabulary and Pronunciation

1. **energy**: strength
2. **health**: good body condition; free from disease
3. **protein**: a substance found in meat or fish
4. **carbohydrates**: nutrients such as sugar and starch that give the body energy

Bread Group

Carbohydrates, Protein, Vitamins

Milk Group

Calcium, Protein, Fats, Minerals

Partial Dictation

Listen and write the word you hear in the blank space. Then decide if you agree or disagree with the statement. Write A for agree and D for disagree next to the sentence.

___ 1. It's important to _____ _____ _____ ____ _____.

___ 2. It's important to have foods from _____ _____ _____ _____ each day.

___ 3. A hamburger with French fries is ____ _____ _____.

___ 4. Bananas, _____, and cherries are examples of _____ _____ _____ .

___ 5. Cheese, milk, and _____ are examples of the _____ group.

___ 6. A healthy dinner would be fish, vegetables, _____, ____ _____.

Discussion

With a partner, decide on some healthy and tasty foods for three meals.

Breakfast	Lunch	Dinner
_____	_____	_____
_____	_____	_____
_____	_____	_____

Food Pantries

Teacher's note:
CD track 38
Full text 133
Instructions for doing the dictation: page 116

Introduction

The United States is the richest country in the world, but there are many poor people who need help. There are food banks in the United States and in many other countries. People who need extra food to feed their families can go and shop in these food banks for food. The food is free.

Vocabulary and Pronunciation

1. **donate**: give either time or money freely
2. **food pantry**: a smaller food bank
3. **volunteer**: work to help, but not get paid
4. **manufacturer**: a business that makes something
5. **spoil**: go bad

Prediction Dictation - Fill in the words you think are correct.

How does a food pantry work?   There is _____ large place where many companies donate food that _____ good, and that they cannot sell. There are farmers who may have extra cucumbers or _____ potatoes or _____ onions. There are food manufacturers that may have _____ cans _____ _____ that they didn't sell. There are big supermarkets that may have _____ food that they did not _____ because they bought too much.

Many restaurants donate _____ that they did not use and which may spoil in a few _____ . Schools, churches, and community centers ask people to _____ food. They will collect it _____ bring it to the food _____ . Sometimes they ask people to bring _____ that are healthy, like peanut butter or tuna fish.

People who need _____ can shop at _____ food pantry when ____ ____ open and there are volunteers there to serve them. And the food is ____.

 Basic Dictations © 2013 Catherine Sadow and Judy DeFilippo

Listening Dictation - Listen and fill in the blank spaces.

How does a food pantry work?   There is _____ large place where many companies donate food that _____ good and that they cannot sell. There are farmers who may have extra cucumbers or _____ potatoes or _____ onions. There are food manufacturers that may have _____ cans _____ _____ that they didn't sell. There are big supermarkets that may have _____ food that they did not _____ because they bought too much.

Many restaurants donate _____ that they did not use and which may spoil in a few _____ . Schools, churches, and community centers ask people to _____ food. They will collect it _____ bring it to the food _____ . Sometimes they ask people to bring _____ that are healthy, like peanut butter or tuna fish.

People who need _____ can shop at _____ food pantry when ____ ____ open and there are volunteers there to serve them. And the food is _____.

Listening

Listen to the conversation and put a check beside the foods you hear in the conversation.

_____ bananas	_____ cans of soup	_____ pasta
_____ bread (white)	_____ cans of baked beans	_____ pasta sauce
_____ bread (sourdough)	_____ jars of peanut butter	_____ rice
_____ bread (wheat)	_____ jars of strawberry jam	_____ potato chips
_____ broccoli	_____ potatoes	_____ noodles
_____ carrots	_____ onions	_____ cookies
_____ cans of tuna fish	_____ French fries	_____ cheese
_____ cans of peaches	_____ Jello	_____ crackers

Discussion

1. Is there a food pantry in your neighborhood?
2. Have you ever worked as a volunteer in your country or in the USA?
3. Why do people give food to a food pantry?

Tipping

Teacher's note:
CD track 39
Full text 135
Instuctions
for doing the
dictation:
page 116

Introduction

In the United States, people tip in restaurants. The restaurant pays the waiter a very low wage. The people who eat at the restaurant pay most of the waiter's wages.

Vocabulary and Pronunciation

1. **salary**: the amount a person earns
2. **tip jar**: a jar that customers can put money in for the server
3. **tip**: extra money for the person who serves you
4. **waiter, waitress**: the person who serves you

Prediction Dictation - Fill in each blank with the word you think are correct.

Peter is having dinner with _____ wife _____ _____ nice restaurant. After _____ finishes his coffee, the waiter gives him his check. It _____ exactly $60.00 and that includes the state tax. Peter adds 15% of $60.00 to the bill. It _____ $9.00. He wants _____ give the _____ $69.00. His _____ says, "He is a good waiter. Give _____ 20%." Peter changes the amount to _____%. It _____ $12.00. He gives the _____ $_____. The _____ says, "_____ _____."

What is the Amount?

Decide what the bill will be after you add the tip.

Amount	15%	Total	or	Amount	20%	Total
$10.00	*#1.50*			$10.00		
$20.00				$20.00		
$30.00				$30.00		
$40.00				$40.00		
$90.00				$90.00		

                    Basic Dictations © 2013 Catherine Sadow and Judy DeFilippo

Listening Dictation - Listen and fill in the blank spaces.

Peter is having dinner with _____ wife _____ _____ nice restaurant. After

_____ finishes his coffee, the waiter gives him his check. It _____ exactly

$60.00 and that includes the state tax. Peter adds 15% of $60.00 to the bill. It

_____ $9.00. He wants _____ give the _____ $69.00. His _____

says, "He is a good waiter. Give _____ 20%." Peter changes the amount to

_____%. It _____ $12.00. He gives the _____ $_____. The

_____ says, "_____ _____."

Listening

Listen to the conversation and put a check beside the people you should tip.

_____ mail carrier   _____ bus driver

_____ taxi driver   _____ sales person

_____ Fed Ex driver   _____ barber

_____ hairdresser

Discussion

1. Do you tip in a restaurant in your country?
2. Who else do you tip in your country?
3. Can you think of other people you tip that are not on the list?
4. What do you do when you see a tip jar?

A Bad Morning

Teacher's note:
CD track 40
Full text 136
Instructions for doing the dictation: page 116

Introduction/Vocabulary/Pronunciation

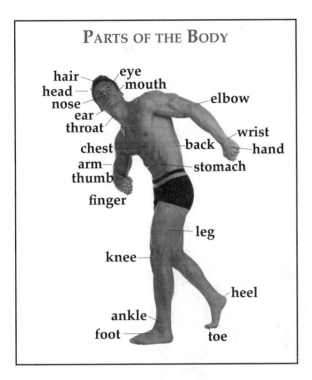

PARTS OF THE BODY

hair, eye, mouth, head, nose, ear, throat, elbow, wrist, back, hand, chest, arm, thumb, stomach, finger, leg, knee, heel, ankle, foot, toe

Henry is having a very bad morning. He doesn't feel well.

Partial Dictation - Listen and fill in the blank spaces.

When Henry wakes up _____ morning, his _____,

_____, and _____ hurt. He also _____ a bad backache. He tells

_____ _____ that he has _____ _____ to work.

His wife takes his temperature. She says, "You are not going _____

_____ _____ . You have a fever of 102 degrees.

"I am going _____ _____ you _____ aspirin, some Vitamin

C, and some _____ chicken soup. If you _____ _____ tomorrow, we

_____ _____ to the doctor. I think _____ _____ the flu."

Listening

Listen to the conversation. Put a check beside the sentences you hear.

_____ 1. "Henry, What's the matter?"
_____ 2. "I have a sore throat."
_____ 3. "I have a stomachache."
_____ 4. "Also my back hurts."
_____ 5. "I can't go to work."
_____ 6. "I've got to go to work."
_____ 7. "I'm going to take your temperature."
_____ 8. "It's 105 degrees."
_____ 9. "Go back to bed."
_____ 10. "I'm going to bring you aspirin, Vitamin C, and hot chicken soup."

Conversion Table	
Fahrenheit	Celsius
99°	37.2°
100	37.8
101	38.3
102	38.9
103	39.4
104	40
105	40.5

98.6° F = normal

102° F = fever

Discussion

1. What do you do if you have a headache?

2. What do you do if you have a stomachache?

3. Do you have some special medicine or food from your country to help you get better?

4. Have you been to a doctor or a hospital in this country?

5. Did the doctor speak your language?

An Appointment for Henry

Teacher's note: CD track 41 Full text 137 Instuctions for doing the dictation: page 116

Introduction

Henry is still sick. He feels terrible and he still has a fever. His wife calls the doctor's office.

Vocabulary

1. **appointment**: an arrangement to meet at a time and place
2. **cancellation**: someone has called to say they cannot come
3. **check up**: a visit to the doctor or dentist to see if you are healthy
4. **degree** (°): temperature measure
5. **emergency**: a dangerous situation
6. **emergency room**: a special place in the hospital for people who are suddenly very sick, or in an accident, and don't have an appointment
7. **fever**: a very high temperature
8. **temperature**: the measurement of heat
9. **Hold on!**: wait

Partial Dictation

Fill in the blank spaces with the words you hear. Then with a partner, read the dialog twice. First you are the secretary. Next you are the wife.

Secretary: Hello. This is Dr. Cutler's office. _____ hold for a minute. I'll be right with you. - - - - - Good morning. Can I help you?

Wife: Good morning. This is Ellen Magill. I need an appointment _____ _____ _____, Henry.

Secretary: Is this for a check up? The next appointment _____ _____ is next month, _____ _____.

Wife: _____, _____ _____ is sick now.

Secretary: If _____ _____ an emergency, he should go to the emergency _____ at the hospital.

Wife: I don't think so. His temperature has been 102 (degrees) for _____ _____. I have given him _____ every _____ _____ but _____ _____ still 102.

Secretary: _____ _____ a cancellation at 2:30 (two thirty) this afternoon. Can _____ _____ _____ at 2:30?

Wife: We _____ _____ _____. Thank you.

Basic Dictations © 2013 Catherine Sadow and Judy DeFilippo

True or False

With a partner, decide if the following statements are True or False.

_____ 1. Henry will go to the emergency room.

_____ 2. His wife says that he is not getting better.

_____ 3. Henry calls the doctor's office.

_____ 4. Henry has not taken any medicine.

_____ 5. Henry will see the doctor the same day his wife speaks to the secretary.

Discussion

1. Have you ever had to make an appointment in English?
2. Is it difficult for you to speak in English on the telephone?
3. Is it difficult for you to understand the person you are speaking to on the telephone because they are speaking English?
4. Do you write everything important down before you call?
5. Do you sometimes have a different person call for you? (a friend or one of your children)
6. With your partner, act out the following situations
   a. You have a toothache. Call the dentist, Dr. Fitch, and make an appointment to see her.
   b. Your child has the flu. Call the office of "Happy Days Pre-School" to tell them that your little girl, Linda, will not be at school today.
   c. You have an important appointment but you don't want your boss to know about it. Call your office and tell them you are sick and can't come to work.

Henry Visits the Doctor

Teacher's note:
CD track 42
Full text 138
Instructions
for doing the
dictation:
page 116

Introduction

Henry still feels terrible. His wife drives him to the doctor's office.

Vocabulary and Pronunciation

1. **a cold**: a cough, a sore throat but no fever
2. **the flu**: a fever, a headache, pain, and very tired
3. **pneumonia**: a serious illness of the lungs
4. **blood**: the red liquid that your heart moves around the body
5. **blood pressure**: how fast blood travels through your body. A good blood pressure reading is 120/65. A high blood pressure reading of 150/100 is not good.
6. **blood pressure cuff**:   (see picture)
7. **pharmacy**: a store where medicines are prepared and sold
8. **prescription**: a paper on which a doctor writes the medicine for a sick person
9. **stethoscope**: The doctor uses this to listen to your heart and lungs. (see the picture on page 74)
10. **urine**: the yellow liquid that comes out of you when you go to the bathroom (pee)
11. **X-ray**: a picture of the inside of your body.

Partial Dictation - Listen and fill in the blank spaces.

First the doctor's assistant _____ Henry's temperature, _____ it _____ _____ degrees. She _____ Henry's blood pressure, and _____ _____ a little high. She takes some blood from Henry, and she _____ _____ to give her some urine. The blood and the urine _____ go to a lab.

Then Dr. Cutler _____ _____ . He asks Henry _____ questions. He listens to Henry's _____ and _____ with his stethoscope. He says to Henry, "I think _____ _____ the flu. I want you _____ _____ _____ to the pharmacy. This is a prescription _____ _____ medicine. Take it _____ _____ _____ _____ with meals. Drink ____ _____ _____ _____ . Get _____ _____ _____ rest. If you _____ _____ _____ by Friday, _____ _____ .

Listening

Listen to the conversation. Circle the correct answer.

Example: The patient's name is Henry Raymond Andrew.

1. Henry's temperature is   **105 degrees   98 degrees   102 degrees**
2   Henry's blood pressure is   **low   a little high   very high**
3. The doctor listens to Henry's heart with a   **stethoscope   x-ray**
4. The doctor gives Henry   **bottle of medicine   prescription**
5. Henry says he feels   **great   terrible   so-so**
6. How old is Henry?   **65   35   45**
7. Henry is going to go to the   **hospital   emergency room   pharmacy**

Discussion

1. Have you ever had a cold? What did you do to get better?
2. Have you ever had the flu? What did you do to get better?
3. Have you ever had a serious illness? What was it?
4. Are doctor visits different in your new country? How?

Dr. Cutler

Name _____ Date _____
Address _____
Phone _____

℞   Take one capsule 4 times
a day for 10 days.

_____
Doctor's Signature

Your Medical History

Teacher's note:
CD track 43
Full text 139
Instuctions
for doing the
dictation:
page 116

Introduction

It's important to know both the internal and external parts of the body. It is also important to know the names of the medical problems people have. Sometimes we have to explain these problems.

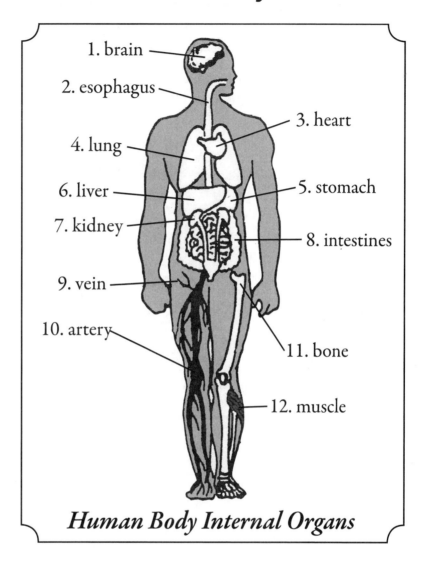

1. brain
2. esophagus
3. heart
4. lung
5. stomach
6. liver
7. kidney
8. intestines
9. vein
10. artery
11. bone
12. muscle

Human Body Internal Organs

Vocabulary and Pronunciation, Part 1

Use your dictionary to understand the vocabulary on this page.

Vocabulary and Pronunciation, Part 2

Diseases/Illnesses	Illnesses	Communicable Diseases
allergies	flu	AIDS
arthritis	fever	measles
asthma	headache/backache	tuberculosis
cancer	diarrhea	STDs
heart trouble	upset stomach	
high blood pressure	sore throat	

   Basic Dictations © 2013 Catherine Sadow and Judy DeFilippo

Partial Dictation

Listen and write the words you hear in the blank space. Then circle the answer you think is correct.

1. You have a headache, a _____, and a _____.
   You have: a. heart trouble   b. the flu   c. diabetes

2. Flowers, animals, _____ dust make you _____ .
   You have: a. an allergy   b. a stomachache   c. diarrhea

3. You are a heavy _____. You started smoking when you were _____.
   You may have: a. lung cancer   b. the flu   c. a fever

4. _____ _____ a temperature of 102°.
   You have: a. heart trouble   b. diarrhea   c. a fever

5. You throw up_____ _____.
   You have: a. an upset stomach   b. an allergy   c. arthritis

Discussion

Discuss the following situations. For vocabulary help, see the box at the bottom of the page.

1. "I am going to have a baby."
   Then you should go to _____.

2. "My baby is sick."
   You should take your baby to _____.

3. "I have a bad toothache."
   You should go to _____.

4. "I think I need new eyeglasses."
   You should see _____.

5. "I am having problems with my husband."
   You should see _____.

| pediatrician | dentist | optician | obstetrician | counselor |

New Patient Registration Form _____

Registration date _____

Please complete this form. If you have any questions, our receptionist will be happy to hekp you.

PERSONAL INFORMATION

Patient's Name   (Last)   (First)   (Middle)

Address	Street	City	State	Zip	Date of Birth	Sex

Telephone Number   Social Security Number

Occupation

Employed by   Business Phone

Please check (✔) any of these problems you have had:

Frequent colds _____
Frequent sore throats _____
Frequent headaches _____
Allergies _____
Stomach problems _____
Kidney problems _____
High blood pressure _____
Anemia _____
Mental depression _____
Serious injuries _____
Heart condition _____

Please check (✔) any of these deseases you have had:

Chicken pox _____
Measles _____
Rubella _____
Mumps _____
Scarlet fever _____
Polio _____
Whooping cough _____
Tuberculosis _____
Diabetes _____
Hepatitis _____
Ulcers _____
Epilepsy _____

Are you taking any medications? _____
Which ones? _____
Are you allergic to any medications? _____
Which ones? _____
Have you had any operations? _____
Please describe them briefly and give the dates: _____
_____

Have you ever been hospitalized for any other reason? _____
Please describe briefly and give the dates: _____
Does anyone have or has anyone in your family had:

                         WHO   RELATION

Diabetes _____ _____ _____
Cancer _____ _____ _____
Heart condition _____ _____ _____

INSURANCE INFORMATION

Name of Subscriber

Address of Subscriber

Name of Insurance company

A Visit to the Dentist

Teacher's note:
CD track 44
Full text 139
Instuctions
for doing the
dictation:
page 116

Introduction/Vocabulary/Pronunciation

Jack is visiting his dentist. He goes every six months. How often do you go?

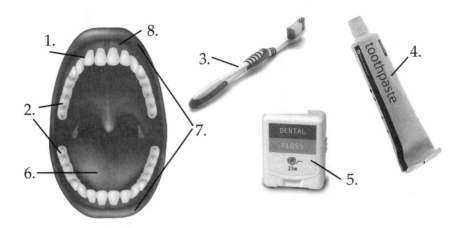

1. **tooth**	2. **teeth**	3. **toothbrush**	4. **toothpaste**
5. **dental floss**	6. **tongue**	7. **lips**	8. **gums**

9. **dental hygienist**: a dentist's helper
10. **X-rays**: pictures of teeth
11. **cavity**: a hole in a tooth
12. **Novocain**: medicine put into the gum for the pain in a tooth

Partial Dictation - Listen and fill in the blank spaces.

Jack went _____ _____ _____ yesterday. He goes every

_____ _____. _____ the dental hygienist cleans _____

_____ and takes a few x-rays. Then the _____, Dr. Fitch,

looks in _____ _____ and says, "_____ _____ a cavity. I'm going

to fill it now." She gives him some Novocain and fills _____ _____.

The dental hygienist gives Jack ____ _____ _____, a

tube of _____, and some dental floss. She says, "_____

_____ _____ _____ _____."

Dictogloss - Listen once, then write what you remember. With a partner, try to reconstruct the sentence.

1.

2.

Listening

Listen to the conversation. Put the sentences in order. Check your answers with your partner and then read the dialog with your partner.

_____ Next Monday, March 19th.

___I___ Hello. This is Jack Black.

_____ Yes, I can. Thank you.

_____ When do you want to come?

_____ I'd like to make an appointment.

_____ Can you come on Tuesday, March 20th, at 4:30?

_____ I'm sorry. The dentist is very busy on Monday.

_____ Goodbye, Jack. We'll see you on Tuesday.

Discussion

1. Why don't some people want to go to the dentist?
2. Is it very expensive to go to a dentist in the United States?
3. Do you have a dentist? How often do you visit your dentist?

Teacher's note:
CD track 45
Full text 140
Instuctions
for doing the
dictation:
page 116

Baby Teeth

Introduction and Vocabulary

Mothers and fathers are very happy when their baby gets its first tooth. They take pictures and tell everyone about it. But they don't think about brushing the baby's teeth.

Vocabulary

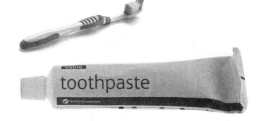

1. **toothbrush**

2. **toothpaste**

3. **cavity:** a hole in a tooth because of decay

4. **toothache:** a pain in a tooth

Pair Dictation, Student A - Dictate to each other.

_____ _____ to get teeth _____ _____ or

ten months old. Dentists say _____ _____ _____ very important ____

_____ your baby's teeth _____ _____ a day. Use just ____

_____ _____ of toothpaste. Babies _____ _____

_____ , but it is important _____ _____ _____.

Pair Dictation, Student B - Dictate to each other.

Babies start _____ _____ _____ at nine _____ _____ _____ _____. _____ _____ that it is _____ _____ to brush _____ _____ _____ two times ____ _____. _____ _____ a little bit _____ _____. _____ won't like it, _____ _____ _____ _____ to do this.

Listening

Listen to the conversation. Put a check beside the sentences you hear.

_____ 1. Why is the baby crying?

_____ 2. He has a headache.

_____ 3. Why are you brushing his teeth?

_____ 4. I never brushed your teeth when you were a baby.

Discussion

1. Do you have "good" teeth or "bad" teeth?

2. Do you use a regular toothbrush or an electric toothbrush?

3. How often do you go to the dentist?

4. Have you ever lost any teeth?

Sleep Like a Baby

Teacher's note:
CD track 46
Full text 140
Instuctions
for doing the
dictation:
page 116

Introduction

Why do we need sleep? Scientists have many ideas, but no one really knows why we need it.

Vocabulary and Pronunciation

1. **light snack**: food not eaten as a meal (a banana, an apple, a piece of bread)
2. **alcohol**: beer, wine, whiskey, etc.
3. **socks**: clothes worn over feet
4. **newborn baby**: a baby who is a few days old
5. **teenagers**: people who are 13 to 19 years old
6. **nap**: a short sleep, not at bedtime

Pair Dictation, Student A - Dictate to each other.

Doctors _____ that we should get _____ _____ _____

_____ of sleep _____ _____. _____ _____ how to

get _____ _____ _____ _____:

1. Don't _____ _____ _____ _____. If you are hungry,

_____ ____ _____ _____.

2. _____ _____ _____ or coffee for _____

_____ before going to sleep.

3. _____ _____ warm socks.

4. Don't watch television _____ _____ _____ just before

going to sleep.

Pair Dictation, Student B - Dictate to each other.

_____ say _____ _____ _____ _____

seven to nine hours _____ _____ every night. This is _____ _____

_____ a good night's sleep:

1. _____ go to bed hungry. _____ _____ _____ _____,

   eat a light snack.

2. Don't drink alcohol _____ _____ _____ four hours _____

   _____ _____ _____.

3. Put on _____ _____.

4. _____ _____ _____ in your bedroom

   _____ _____ _____ _____ _____ .

Discussion

1. What time do you usually go to bed? During the week? On the weekend?
2. What time do you usually get up? During the week? On the weekend?
3. Do you sometimes take naps?
4. Do you dream? Do you sometimes remember your dreams?
5. Do you like to sleep?
6. Match the ages with the amount of sleep needed. How much sleep is important for each of these people?

   _____ newborn baby   a. 7-8 hours
   _____ 1-12 month old baby   b. 11-13 hours
   _____ 1-3 year old   c. 12-15 hours
   _____ 5-12 year old   d. 18 hours
   _____ teenagers   e. 9-10 hours
   _____ adults (including older people) f. 14-19 hours

Infant Immunizations

Teacher's
note:
CD track 47
Full text 140
Instuctions
for doing the
dictation:
page 116

Introduction

All children must get vaccinations to stay healthy. Doctors start to vaccinate babies when they are about two months old.

Vocabulary and Pronunciation

1. **communicable**: it is easy to catch (the disease from another person)
2. **injection, shot, inoculation**: The doctor puts the medicine (the vaccine) in an arm with a needle.
3. **infant**: young baby
4. **immunize**: to stop the person from getting the disease
5. **immunization card**: a record of your immunizations
6. **vaccine**: the medicine that stops the person from getting the disease

IMMUNIZATION CARD	VACCINE	DATE GIVEN	DOCTOR'S OFFICE OR CLINIC
Name: _____	Polio	5/18	
	Polio	7/18	
Birthday: _____			
Allergies: _____	DTP/Td	10/20	
Vaccine Reactions: _____			
RETAIN THIS DOCUMENT	MMR	7/21	

Dictogloss - Listen once, then write what you remember. With a partner, try to reconstruct the sentence.

1.

2.

Partial Dictation - Listen and fill in the blank spaces.

In many states _____ must have some vaccinations

_____ they can go _____ _____. This is a law. The vaccines

protect _____ from getting communicable diseases. Communicable means

that _____ _____ _____ has a disease, many others _____

_____ _____ from that person.

For example, seventy _____ ago many children _____ polio and

_____ children died. Everyone _____ afraid _____ _____. Now, because

there is a polio _____, polio is almost gone _____ _____

_____ _____.

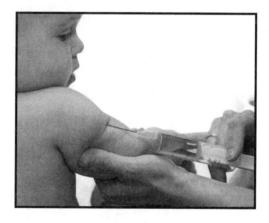

These are some of the vaccines that infants and young children get:

Small pox
DPT (diphtheria, pertussis -- also called whooping cough -- and tetanus)
Polio
MMR (measles, mumps and rubella – also called German measles)

Discussion

1. Why do you think it is important that everyone is inoculated?
2. There are some countries where many people still get polio. Why?

Teacher's note:
CD track 47
Full text 141
Instuctions
for doing the
dictation:
page 116

How Much Do They Make?

Introduction

The salaries in this unit are annual salaries. Annual salaries are yearly salaries. In the graph, the salaries are average yearly salaries. They are neither the highest nor the lowest.

Vocabulary and Pronunciation

Part 1 Talk about the different occupations.

She is a teacher.   They are _____.   He is _____.   She is _____.

They are _____.   She is _____.   He is _____.   He is _____.

Part 2 Match column A with column B

A	B
1. A mechanic	a. heals patients
2. A hair stylist	b. flies planes
3. A pilot	c. fixes cars
4. A policeman	d. sings and acts
5. A teacher	e. directs traffic
6. A plumber	f. teaches
7. A rock star	g. cuts hair
8. A doctor	h. repairs sinks

Part 3   Practice the pronunciation of these numbers.

$100	$1000	$10,000	$100,000	$1,000,000
300	3,000	12,000	200,000	2,000,000
500	5,600	15,000	500.000	5,000,000
800	8,000	33,000	700,000	8,000,000
950	9,500	57,000	825,000	9,500,000

Vocabulary and Pronunciation

Part 3 Study the chart and the salaries of these occupations. Practice pronouncing the salaries of each person.

AVERAGE YEARLY SALARY

OCCUPATION	30,000	40,000	50,000	60,000	70,000	80,000	90,000	100,000	110,000	120,000	130,000	140,000	150,000	160,000
Policeman														
Doctor														
Teacher														
Plumber														
Rock star														
Hairstylist														
Pilot														
Mechanic														

Partial Dictation

Part 1 Listen and write the salary.

1. I am a _____ . My annual salary is _____.

2. She is a _____ . Her average salary is _____ .

3. I am a _____ stylist. I receive about _____ a year.

4. The average _____ salary of a pilot is _____.

5. Most _____ _____ make an annual salary of about

   _____.

Basic Dictations © 2013 Catherine Sadow and Judy DeFilippo

Partial Dictation

Part 2 Listen and write. Then decide if the answer is "True" (T) or "False"(F).

_____ 1. A pilot's average _____ is _____ than a teacher's.

_____ 2. A _____ annual salary _____ _____ $65,00 year.

_____ 3. A _____ and a _____ make about _____

_____.

_____ 4. A _____ _____ salary is _____ _____ $200,000

a year.

_____ 5. A doctor makes the same _____ _____ as a _____

_____.

Discussion

Part 1 Work with a partner and answer these questions. There are 52 weeks in a year.

1. The above salaries are yearly salaries. Many people get a weekly salary. If mechanics make $52,000 a year, how much do they make a week?
2. If a pilot's salary is $100,000 a year, how much do they make a week?
3. If a rock star makes $3,000,000 a year, how much do they make in a week? A day?
4. You make $500 a week. What is your yearly salary? Is that a good salary?
5. Name five occupations with high salaries in your country.
6. Name five occupations with low salaries in your country.
7. What is your dream salary?

Part 2 How many can you name?

1. Name someone who works with children. (can you name four occupations?)
2. Name someone who wears a uniform at work. (can you name four?)
3. Name someone who works at a dangerous job.
4. Name someone who works in a restaurant.
5. Name someone who works in a hospital.

Looking for a Job

Teacher's note:
CD track 49
Full text 141
Instuctions for doing the dictation: page 116

Introduction

Sara Soto is looking for a job. She is from Guatemala in Central America. At home she was an office manager. She is learning English in the United States and would like a job in San Antonio when her English improves. She is searching the Internet for jobs in her area.

Vocabulary and Pronunciation

1. **part time**: about 20 hours of work per week; full time is 40 hours per week
2. **superintendent**: the top position in a school system
3. **qualifications**: the abilities and background that you have to do the job
4. **training**: teaching someone a job
5. **experience**: where you worked before and for how long
6. **benefits**: extra services a company provides (medical insurance/pension)

Prediction Dictation - Fill in the words you think are correct.

Sara Soto has two children ages seven and twelve. She wants _____ find a part-time job while _____ children are in school. _____ doesn't want to work on weekends or _____ the summer.

First, _____ thinks about what she can do. _____ she thinks about what she likes _____ do. She likes to drive, _____ she thinks she _____ get a special driver's _____ to drive a school bus. This way she can work while her _____ are in school.

To apply for this _____ of job, she can call _____ superintendent's office of the _____ Antonio Public Schools or a school system in a nearby town and ask if there _____ any openings for school bus drivers. She _____ ask about the qualifications _____ training, too. What are some other ways that Sara can _____ a part-time job?

Listening Dictation - Listen and fill in the blank spaces.

Sara Soto has two children ages seven and twelve. She wants _____ find a part-time job while _____ children are in school. _____ doesn't want to work on weekends or _____ the summer.

First, _____ thinks about what she can do. _____ she thinks about what she likes _____ do. She likes to drive, _____ she thinks she _____ get a special driver's _____ to drive a school bus. This way she can work while her _____ are in school.

To apply for this _____ of job, she can call _____ superintendent's office of the _____ Antonio Public Schools or a school system in a nearby town and ask if there _____ any openings for school bus drivers. She _____ ask about the qualifications _____ training, too. What are some other ways that Sara can _____ a part-time job?

Discussion

GENERAL HELP WANTED

NURSES AIDES
Will train; full time only
Work with the elderly
North Shore Nursing Home
Call for appt. 788-438-0981

BAKER'S HELPER
Zeppy's Bagel Company
4:00   AM to 12 NOON
No experience necessary
Apply in person only
753 Main St. San Antonio

SCHOOL BUS DRIVER
with a Class II license and a good
driving record. We offer a good
starting salary and good benefits.
Call the Superintendent's Office:
San Antonio: 443-5688

CASHIERS AT CVS
Will train. Immediate full and
part time openings. Dependable
and trustworthy. Come in and
fill out application. Good salary
and benefits. 717 Water St.
San Antonio

Take turns asking and answering the questions.

Student A: What job are you interested in?

Student B: _____.

Student A: What is the name of the company?

Student B: _____.

Student A: Do you need to have any experience?

Student B: _____.

Student A: What do you think is a good salary for the job? ($$ per hour)

Student B: _____.

Student A: How do you contact the company?

Student B: _____.

Student A: Do you think you'll apply for the job? Why or why not?

Student B: _____.

An Application Form

It is a good idea to write at home all of the information to fill out employment applications. Take the sheet with you and use it when you have to fill out an application. Fill out this form and save it to use later.

PERSONAL AND EMPLOYMENT FACT SHEET

Personal Data

Name _____ Social Security Number _____

Address _____ How long at this address _____

_____

Telephone _____

Marital status _____

Dependents (indicate ages of any children) _____

Education

	Name and address	Date attended	Courses
Elementary School			
High School			
Trade or Business School			
College			

Special Skills (licenses or trades) _____

Previous Jobs (list latest job first)

From-To dates	Name and Address of Employer	Supervisor	Position held and Salary	Reason for Leaving

References

		Name and address	Telephone Number
Personal	1.		
	2.		
	3.		
Business	1.		
	2.		
	3.		

Social Security

Teacher's note:
CD track 5
Full text 142
Instuctions for doing the dictation: page 116

Introduction

If you work in the United States, some of the money you make will go to Social Security (FICA). When you are older (65 years old) and you retire, you will receive money every month. It comes from the government, but it is your money. Both you and your employer give this money to the government when you are working. You will get it when you are old and need it.

Vocabulary

1. **Social Security card**: the card you get in order to work in the United States
2. **Social Security number**: the nine-digit number that is on the card
3. **FICA**: Federal Insurance Contributions Act
4. **employer**: the person you work for
5. **to retire**: stop working

Prediction Dictation - Fill in the words you think are correct.

Everyone in the United _____ who works has _____ Social Security card

and _____ Social Security number. Your employer takes money out of your paycheck

and gives it _____ the government. You get money back when you _____, or

_____ you are too sick _____ work.

To get _____ card and _____number, go _____ a Social Security Office and fill out a

form. Call the _____ or go on the Internet (SocialSecurity.org) to see what

you need to bring with _____ . For example, you may need to bring a passport, a

birth certificate, or a Green _____ .

Basic Dictations © 2013 Catherine Sadow and Judy DeFilippo

Listening Dictation - Listen and fill in the blank spaces.

Everyone in the United _____ who works has _____ Social Security

card and _____ Social Security number. Your employer takes money out of your

paycheck and gives it _____ the government. You get money back when you

_____, or _____ you are too sick _____ work.

To get _____ card and _____number, go _____ a Social Security Office and fill

out a form. Call the _____ or go on the Internet (SocialSecurity.org) to

see what you need to bring with _____ . For example, you may need to bring a

passport, a birth certificate, or a Green _____ .

Listening

Listen to the caller. Answer the questions. Then check your answers with a partner.

1. Does Francisco have to wait before he can talk to a representative? Why?
2. What does Francisco want to know?
3. What two things does the representative want to know?
4. Where is Francisco from?
5. What must he bring to the Social Security Office?
6. How much will it cost?

Discussion

1. Do you know if you need a special form in your country in order to work?
2. If you have been to a Social Security Office, tell your partner about it.
3. There is a form that you fill out when you need a Social Security card and number. Look at the form on the next page and discuss it with a partner. See if you can fill out the form.

SOCIAL SECURITY ADMINISTRATION
Application for a Social Security Card

Form Approved
OMB No. 0960-0066

1

NAME TO BE SHOWN ON CARD	First	Full Middle Name	Last
FULL NAME AT BIRTH IF OTHER THAN ABOVE	First	Full Middle Name	Last
OTHER NAMES USED			

2 Social Security number previously assigned to the person listed in item 1 □□□ – □□ – □□□□

3 PLACE OF BIRTH _____ (Do Not Abbreviate) City — State or Foreign Country

Office Use Only — FCI

4 DATE OF BIRTH _____ MM/DD/YYYY

5 CITIZENSHIP (Check One)
□ U.S. Citizen
□ Legal Alien Allowed To Work
□ Legal Alien Not Allowed To Work (See Instructions On Page 3)
□ Other (See Instructions On Page 3)

6 ETHNICITY
Are You Hispanic or Latino?
(Your Response is Voluntary)
□ Yes □ No

7 RACE
Select One or More
(Your Response is Voluntary)
□ Native Hawaiian □ American Indian □ Other Pacific Islander
□ Alaska Native □ Black/African American □ White
□ Asian

8 SEX □ Male □ Female

9

A. PARENT/ MOTHER'S NAME AT HER BIRTH	First	Full Middle Name	Last

B. PARENT/ MOTHER'S SOCIAL SECURITY NUMBER (See instructions for 9 B on Page 3) □□□ – □□ – □□□□ □ Unknown

10

A. PARENT/ FATHER'S NAME	First	Full Middle Name	Last

B. PARENT/ FATHER'S SOCIAL SECURITY NUMBER (See instructions for 10B on Page 3) □□□ – □□ – □□□□ □ Unknown

11 Has the person listed in item 1 or anyone acting on his/her behalf ever filed for or received a Social Security number card before?
□ Yes (If "yes" answer questions 12-13) □ No □ Don't Know (If "don't know," skip to question 14.)

12 Name shown on the most recent Social Security card issued for the person listed in item 1
First — Full Middle Name — Last

13 Enter any different date of birth if used on an earlier application for a card _____ MM/DD/YYYY

14 TODAY'S DATE _____ MM/DD/YYYY

15 DAYTIME PHONE NUMBER ( ) – Area Code — Number

16 MAILING ADDRESS (Do Not Abbreviate)
Street Address, Apt. No., PO Box, Rural Route No.
City — State/Foreign Country — ZIP Code

I declare under penalty of perjury that I have examined all the information on this form, and on any accompanying statements or forms, and it is true and correct to the best of my knowledge.

17 YOUR SIGNATURE

18 YOUR RELATIONSHIP TO THE PERSON IN ITEM 1 IS:
□ Self □ Natural Or Adoptive Parent □ Legal Guardian □ Other (Specify) _____

DO NOT WRITE BELOW THIS LINE (FOR SSA USE ONLY)

NPN			DOC	NTI	CAN		ITV
PBC	EVI	EVA	EVC	PRA	NWR	DNR	UNIT

EVIDENCE SUBMITTED	SIGNATURE AND TITLE OF EMPLOYEE(S) REVIEWING EVIDENCE AND/OR CONDUCTING INTERVIEW
	DATE
	DCL — DATE

Form **SS-5-FS** (08-2011) ef (08-2011) Destroy Prior Editions   Page 5

The Pay Slip

Teacher's note:
CD track 51
Full text 143
Instuctions
for doing the
dictation:
page 116

Introduction

CD track 51
Full text 143

When we work, we get paid. Sometimes it is every week. Sometimes it is every two weeks. Sometimes it is once a month. However, we do not get all that we earn. Some money goes to our Social Security (FICA). Some money goes to the national government (federal tax). Some money goes to the state if your state has a state tax. Some money may go for medical insurance.

Vocabulary and Pronunciation

1. **deductions**: money taken out of your pay
2. **FICA**: Social Security Insurance (the money you get when you retire} and Medicare contribution (healthcare you get when you retire)
3. **federal tax**: the money you pay to the government
4. **IRS (Internal Revenue Service)**: tax office
5. **state tax**: the money you pay to the state (Not all states have a state tax.)
6. **pay slip**: the paper you receive with your pay explaining what you earned and what was taken out. It can also be called a Pay Stub.
7. **gross pay**: what you earn before deductions
8. **net pay**: what you receive after the deductions

Partial Dictation - Listen and fill in the blank spaces.

Frank is _____ . He is _____ _____ . Jobs are not easy _____
_____ , but he has a _____ . He _____ _____ for a company
that _____ furniture.

Every _____ he gets _____ _____ for $480, or more if _____ _____
overtime. He also gets a statement of earnings and deductions. _____ _____
important for him to keep this.

He is going _____ _____ full-time for _____ _____. He is saving
_____ _____ so _____ _____ _____ to community college.

Discussion, Part 1

1. Why is Frank only planning to work for 15 months?
2. Do you think this is a good plan? Why or why not?
3. With your partner look at Frank's pay slip and answer the questions that follow.

Richford's Furniture

Employee's Statement of Earnings and Deductions – Detach and Retain

Period Ending ___July 30___

Name ___Frank O'Leary___

$12.00	Regular Hours	40	$480	00
$18.00	Overtime Hours	5	$90	00
Total Earnings			$570	00
FICA		$34	20	
Fed. Income Tax		$57	00	
5% State Inc. Tax		$28	50	
Blue Cross (B/C)		$42	00	
Total Deductions			$161	70
NET PAY			$408	30

1. Frank makes _____ an hour.
2. Frank makes _____ an hour when he works overtime.
3. Frank worked _____ hours during the week ending July 30.
4. His total earnings or salary before anything was deducted was _____.
5. His net pay (take-home pay) was _____.
6. He paid _____ to Social Security.
7. He paid _____ to federal income taxes.
8. He paid _____ to state income taxes.
9. He paid _____ for medical insurance.
10. His total deductions were _____

Discussion, Part 2

Frank pays Federal income tax. His employer takes it out of his paycheck and gives it to the government. Before April 15th of each year, Frank has to fill out a form to send to the IRS (Internal Revenue Service). When he fills out the form he will learn if he has to give the government more money or if the government has to return money to him (a refund). Have you ever filled out an income tax form for the IRS? Was it difficult?

There is a form on the next page. Discuss it with your teacher.

Form **1040** U.S. Individual Income Tax Return

Department of the Treasury—Internal Revenue Service (99)

2012 OMB No. 1545-0074 IRS Use Only—Do not write or staple in this space.

For the year Jan. 1–Dec. 31, 2012, or other tax year beginning , 2012, ending , 20

See separate instructions.

Your first name and initial	Last name		Your social security number
If a joint return, spouse's first name and initial	Last name		Spouse's social security number

Home address (number and street). If you have a P.O. box, see instructions. | Apt. no.

▲ Make sure the SSN(s) above and on line 6c are correct.

City, town or post office, state, and ZIP code. If you have a foreign address, also complete spaces below (see instructions).

Presidential Election Campaign
Check here if you, or your spouse if filing jointly, want $3 to go to this fund. Checking a box below will not change your tax or refund. ☐ You ☐ Spouse

Foreign country name	Foreign province/state/county	Foreign postal code

Filing Status
Check only one box.

1 ☐ Single
2 ☐ Married filing jointly (even if only one had income)
3 ☐ Married filing separately. Enter spouse's SSN above and full name here. ▶
4 ☐ Head of household (with qualifying person). (See instructions.) If the qualifying person is a child but not your dependent, enter this child's name here. ▶
5 ☐ Qualifying widow(er) with dependent child

Exemptions

6a ☐ **Yourself.** If someone can claim you as a dependent, **do not** check box 6a . . . . . .
b ☐ **Spouse** . . . .

c **Dependents:**

(1) First name Last name	(2) Dependent's social security number	(3) Dependent's relationship to you	(4) ✓ if child under age 17 qualifying for child tax credit (see instructions)
			☐
			☐
			☐
			☐

If more than four dependents, see instructions and check here ▶ ☐

d Total number of exemptions claimed . . . .

Boxes checked on 6a and 6b

No. of children on 6c who:
• lived with you
• did not live with you due to divorce or separation (see instructions)

Dependents on 6c not entered above

Add numbers on lines above ▶

Income

Attach Form(s) W-2 here. Also attach Forms W-2G and 1099-R if tax was withheld.

If you did not get a W-2, see instructions.

Enclose, but do not attach, any payment. Also, please use Form 1040-V.

7	Wages, salaries, tips, etc. Attach Form(s) W-2	7
8a	Taxable interest. Attach Schedule B if required	8a
b	Tax-exempt interest. Do not include on line 8a . . .	8b	
9a	Ordinary dividends. Attach Schedule B if required	9a
b	Qualified dividends	9b	
10	Taxable refunds, credits, or offsets of state and local income taxes . . .	10
11	Alimony received	11
12	Business income or (loss). Attach Schedule C or C-EZ	12
13	Capital gain or (loss). Attach Schedule D if required. If not required, check here ▶ ☐	13
14	Other gains or (losses). Attach Form 4797	14
15a	IRA distributions .	15a	b Taxable amount . . .	15b
16a	Pensions and annuities	16a	b Taxable amount . . .	16b
17	Rental real estate, royalties, partnerships, S corporations, trusts, etc. Attach Schedule E	17
18	Farm income or (loss). Attach Schedule F	18
19	Unemployment compensation	19
20a	Social security benefits	20a	b Taxable amount . . .	20b
21	Other income. List type and amount		21
22	Combine the amounts in the far right column for lines 7 through 21. This is your **total income** ▶	22

Adjusted Gross Income

23	Educator expenses	23		
24	Certain business expenses of reservists, performing artists, and fee-basis government officials. Attach Form 2106 or 2106-EZ	24		
25	Health savings account deduction. Attach Form 8889	25		
26	Moving expenses. Attach Form 3903	26		
27	Deductible part of self-employment tax. Attach Schedule SE	27		
28	Self-employed SEP, SIMPLE, and qualified plans . .	28		
29	Self-employed health insurance deduction	29		
30	Penalty on early withdrawal of savings	30		
31a	Alimony paid b Recipient's SSN ▶	31a		
32	IRA deduction	32		
33	Student loan interest deduction	33		
34	Tuition and fees. Attach Form 8917	34		
35	Domestic production activities deduction. Attach Form 8903	35		
36	Add lines 23 through 35		36	
37	Subtract line 36 from line 22. This is your **adjusted gross income** ▶		37	

For Disclosure, Privacy Act, and Paperwork Reduction Act Notice, see separate instructions.   Cat. No. 11320B   Form **1040** (2012)

Form 1040 (2012) | Page **2**

Tax and Credits	38	Amount from line 37 (adjusted gross income)		38
	39a	Check if: ☐ **You** were born before January 2, 1948, ☐ Blind. ☐ **Spouse** was born before January 2, 1948, ☐ Blind. } Total boxes checked ▶ 39a		
Standard Deduction for —	b	If your spouse itemizes on a separate return or you were a dual-status alien, check here▶ 39b☐		
• People who check any box on line 39a or 39b or who can be claimed as a dependent, see instructions.	40	**Itemized deductions** (from Schedule A) or your **standard deduction** (see left margin)		40
	41	Subtract line 40 from line 38		41
	42	**Exemptions.** Multiply $3,800 by the number on line 6d		42
	43	**Taxable income.** Subtract line 42 from line 41. If line 42 is more than line 41, enter -0-		43
	44	**Tax** (see instructions). Check if any from: a ☐ Form(s) 8814 b ☐ Form 4972 c ☐ 962 election		44
• All others: Single or Married filing separately, $5,950	45	**Alternative minimum tax** (see instructions). Attach Form 6251		45
	46	Add lines 44 and 45 ▶		46
Married filing jointly or Qualifying widow(er), $11,900	47	Foreign tax credit. Attach Form 1116 if required	47	
	48	Credit for child and dependent care expenses. Attach Form 2441	48	
	49	Education credits from Form 8863, line 19	49	
Head of household, $8,700	50	Retirement savings contributions credit. Attach Form 8880	50	
	51	Child tax credit. Attach Schedule 8812, if required	51	
	52	Residential energy credits. Attach Form 5695	52	
	53	Other credits from Form: a ☐ 3800 b ☐ 8801 c ☐	53	
	54	Add lines 47 through 53. These are your **total credits**		54
	55	Subtract line 54 from line 46. If line 54 is more than line 46, enter -0- ▶		55
Other Taxes	56	Self-employment tax. Attach Schedule SE		56
	57	Unreported social security and Medicare tax from Form: a ☐ 4137 b ☐ 8919		57
	58	Additional tax on IRAs, other qualified retirement plans, etc. Attach Form 5329 if required		58
	59a	Household employment taxes from Schedule H		59a
	b	First-time homebuyer credit repayment. Attach Form 5405 if required		59b
	60	Other taxes. Enter code(s) from instructions		60
	61	Add lines 55 through 60. This is your **total tax** ▶		61
Payments	62	Federal income tax withheld from Forms W-2 and 1099	62	
	63	2012 estimated tax payments and amount applied from 2011 return	63	
If you have a qualifying child, attach Schedule EIC.	64a	**Earned income credit (EIC)**	64a	
	b	Nontaxable combat pay election 64b		
	65	Additional child tax credit. Attach Schedule 8812	65	
	66	American opportunity credit from Form 8863, line 8	66	
	67	Reserved	67	
	68	Amount paid with request for extension to file	68	
	69	Excess social security and tier 1 RRTA tax withheld	69	
	70	Credit for federal tax on fuels. Attach Form 4136	70	
	71	Credits from Form: a ☐ 2439 b ☐ Reserved c ☐ 8801 d ☐ 8885	71	
	72	Add lines 62, 63, 64a, and 65 through 71. These are your **total payments** ▶		72
Refund	73	If line 72 is more than line 61, subtract line 61 from line 72. This is the amount you **overpaid**		73
	74a	Amount of line 73 you want **refunded to you.** If Form 8888 is attached, check here ▶ ☐		74a
Direct deposit? ▶ See instructions.	b	Routing number ▶c Type: ☐ Checking ☐ Savings		
	d	Account number		
	75	Amount of line 73 you want **applied to your 2013 estimated tax** ▶ 75		
Amount You Owe	76	**Amount you owe.** Subtract line 72 from line 61. For details on how to pay, see instructions ▶		76
	77	Estimated tax penalty (see instructions) 77		

Third Party Designee — Do you want to allow another person to discuss this return with the IRS (see instructions)? ☐ **Yes.** Complete below. ☐ **No**

Designee's name ▶ ___ Phone no. ▶ ___ Personal identification number (PIN) ▶ ☐☐☐☐☐

Sign Here — Under penalties of perjury, I declare that I have examined this return and accompanying schedules and statements, and to the best of my knowledge and belief, they are true, correct, and complete. Declaration of preparer (other than taxpayer) is based on all information of which preparer has any knowledge.

Joint return? See instructions. Keep a copy for your records.

Your signature	Date	Your occupation	Daytime phone number
Spouse's signature. If a joint return, **both** must sign.	Date	Spouse's occupation	If the IRS sent you an Identity Protection PIN, enter it here (see inst.) ☐☐☐☐☐☐

Paid Preparer Use Only

Print/Type preparer's name	Preparer's signature	Date	Check ☐ if self-employed	PTIN
Firm's name ▶			Firm's EIN ▶	
Firm's address ▶			Phone no.	

Form **1040** (2012)

Teacher's note:
CD track 52
Full text 144
Instuctions
for doing the
dictation:
page 116

Banks and Bank Accounts

Introduction

Today people pay bills in different ways. They pay bills online. They pay bills with their credit cards. However there are many important reasons to have a bank account.

Vocabulary and Pronunciation

1. **ATM**: a machine where you can withdraw cash from your account
2. **credit card**: You buy something with it and pay later.
3. **debit card**: You buy something and the money is taken out of your account.
4. **deposit**: to put in
5. **direct deposit**: money put into your account by an employer
6. **joint account**: the same bank account for two people (husband and wife)
7. **salary**: the money you earn at a job
8. **withdraw**: to take out

Partial Dictation - Listen and fill in the blank spaces.

If you _____ , it is important _____ _____ a checking account _____ _____ _____ . Most employers will _____ your salary _____ your _____ account by direct deposit.

You _____ withdraw money by writing a check, by using a _____ debit _____, or by using an _____ . If you _____ _____ _____ a large item like a _____, you may _____ to your _____ to get a loan.

Listening

Listen to the conversation and answer the following questions. Check your answers with a partner.

1. The bank employee was
   a. not friendly
   b. polite
   c. sad

2. The student wanted to open
   a. a checking account
   b. a savings account
   c. a checking account and a savings account

3. All of the bank officers were
   a. having lunch
   b. busy
   c. using their computers

4. He needed
   a. a telephone bill
   b. one ID
   c. an ID with his picture on it

5. The bank employee asked him
   a. to wait
   b. if he would like a cup of coffee
   c. to come back tomorrow

Discussion

1. Do you have a bank account? Was it easy or hard to open it?
2. When you go to the bank, is there someone there who can speak your first language?
3. When you get mail from the bank about your account, is it hard to read it?
4. Do you do your banking online?
5. Do you think that banks can make mistakes?

Writing Checks

Teacher's note:
CD track 53
Full text 144
Instuctions
for doing the
dictation:
page 116

Introduction

We use our credit cards often and we also pay some of our bills on the internet. There are also times when we have to write a check.

Vocabulary and Pronunciation

1. **joint checking account**: an account for more than one person
2. **direct deposit**: your employer puts money into your account
3. **employer**: the person you work for

Partial Dictation - Listen and fill in the blank spaces.

Henry _____ _____ _____ Maryanne, both _____ . At the end of

_____ _____ their employers _____ _____ into their joint

checking account by direct deposit.

They _____ their credit cards _____ _____ _____ they

buy _____ _____ . At the end of every month, _____ _____

_____ together to write checks _____ their other bills. These are

_____ of the checks they write _____ _____ : the gas company,

the electric company, the rent, and medical bills. _____ _____ very careful

to write down the amount of _____ _____ in their checkbook.

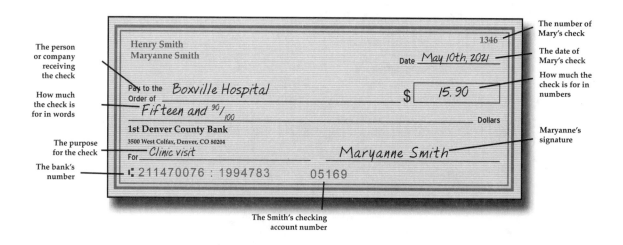

Discussion

With a partner, discuss the following.

1. Do you write many checks or do you pay many bills using the Internet?
2. With your partner, look at this check and then answer the questions that follow.

a. What is the check number? _____

b. Who is going to receive the check? _____

c. How much is the check for? _____

d. What is the check for? _____

e. What is the date of the check? _____

f. What is the checking account number? _____

g. Who signed the check? _____

3. In the blank check below, pay the dentist, Dr. Fitch, $110.00.

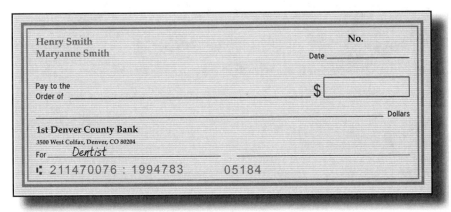

Teacher's note:
CD track 54
Full text 145
Instructions
for doing the
dictation:
page 116

Henry Drives to Work

Introduction

Henry needs a car to get to work. He often works at night.

Vocabulary and Pronunciation, Part 1

1. **seatbelt**: a belt you put on in the car to keep yourself safe
2. **to park**: to put a car in a place and then leave it
3. **parking lot**: the place where you leave a car
4. **emergency room**: a part of a hospital for people who have been hurt in accidents or who are suddenly very sick

Vocabulary and Pronunciation, Part 2 - Practice saying each part..

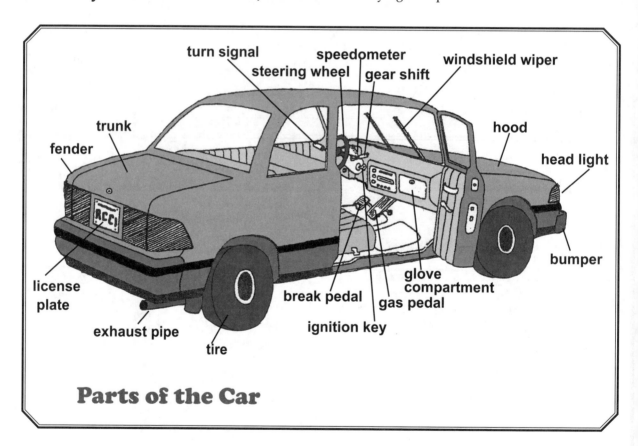

Parts of the Car

Vocabulary and Pronunciation, Part 3

Pronounce the words in the box, and put them in the sentences.

speedometer	brake	windshield wipers	headlights
	gas pedal	ignition key	

1. I turn on the _____ when it is raining.
2. I turn on the _____ when it gets dark.
3. I turn the _____ to start my car.
4. When I want to go faster. I put my foot on the _____.
5. When I stop at a red light, I put my foot on the _____.
6. The _____ says that I'm going 60 miles an hour.

Partial Dictation - Listen and fill in the blank spaces.

Henry is a _____ _____ driver. When he _____ _____ his car, he _____ ____ his seatbelt. He _____ _____ _____ into the ignition and _____ the car. It is raining, so he _____ _____ the windshield wipers. It is almost dark, so he _____ _____ the headlights. He _____ _____ _____ on the gas pedal and begins to drive to his night job at the hospital. Soon he comes to a _____ sign. He _____ _____ _____ on the brake and _____ _____ _____. In _____ minutes he is at the hospital and _____ _____ _____ in the parking lot. Henry _____ in the emergency room in the hospital, and sometimes he has _____ _____ at night.

 Basic Dictations © 2013 Catherine Sadow and Judy DeFilippo

Discussion

1. When do you turn on the windshield wipers?
2. When do you put your key into the ignition?
3. When do you turn on the headlights?
4. What do you do if you want to stop the car?
5. What tells you how fast you are going?
6. How do you start the car?
7. Can you drive? How old were you when you learned to drive?
8. Who taught you to drive?
9. Do you drive a car to school or to work?
10. Do you work at night or go to school at night?

Fifty Minutes on the Road

Teacher's note:
CD track 55
Full text 145
Instuctions for doing the dictation: page 116

Introduction

How long does it take you to get to work or school? Do you enjoy that time?

Vocabulary and Pronunciation

1. **% (percent)**: .50 = 50 percent = ½ (one half)
2. **under the age of 10**: less than 10 years old
3. **over the age of 10**: more than 10
4. **lipstick**: color for the lips, often red or pink
5. **passenger**: a person who is riding in the car but not driving

Partial Dictation 1 - Listen and fill in the blank spaces.

Fifty minutes _____ the average total _____ an American worker

travels from _____ to _____ every day. Most people drive. Some

_____ ride their bicycles. Others take a _____ or train.

Listen and Write

Look at the chart "How Americans get to work." Talk about the ways Americans get to work. Listen for the percentages and write them in the correct box. One box "under age 55" is for the percentage of that group of people. The other box "over 55" is for the other age group. The first one is done for you.

How Americans get to work	under 55	over 55
1 person in a car 🚗 🚶	76.6%	
Carpool 🚗 🚶🚶🚶🚶		7.3%
Public transportation 🚌		
Walk 🚶	2.8%	
Taxi, motorbike, bicycle 🚕 🏍 🚲		
Work at home 🏠		

Basic Dictations © 2013 Catherine Sadow and Judy DeFilippo

Discussion

Read your answers out loud. Try to use complete sentences.
For example: Four percent of the people who are over the age of 55 take public transportation.

1. _____ of the people who are <u>over</u> 55 work at home.
2. _____ of the people who are <u>under</u> 55 take public transportation.
3. _____ of the people who are <u>over</u> 55 walk to work.
4. _____ of the people who are <u>over</u> 55 take taxis or motorbikes to work.
5. _____ of the people who are <u>under</u> 55 carpool.

Partial Dictation 2 - Listen and fill in the blank spaces.

What do we do on our way _____ _____? 96% (ninety-six percent) say that

they _____ to other passengers. _____ say that they _____ their

breakfast or _____ coffee or tea. _____ use a _____ _____,

and _____ say that they sometimes _____ their _____ or

_____ _____ lipstick. Some people listen to _____ or the news.

Discussion

1. How long does it take you to get to work or school?
2. What things do you do while you're on your way to work or school?
3. Would you like to work at home?
4. If you listen to music on the way, what kind of music do you listen to?

Henry's Accident

Teacher's note:
CD track 56
Full text 146
Instuctions
for doing the
dictation:
page 116

Introduction

Car accidents happen every day. Some are serious and people have to go to the hospital. Most of them are not serious.

Vocabulary and Pronunciation

1. **fault**: a mistake
2. **license**: The card you have with you when you're driving. It has your name, address, birth date, and license number.
3. **serious**: bad or dangerous
4. **suddenly**: quickly
5. **registration**: an important paper with information about your car

Partial Dictation - Listen and fill in the blank spaces.

Henry is driving _____ _____ _____ at the hospital. He _____

the _____ sign. He _____ _____ _____ on the brake pedal

and stops. The car behind him _____ _____ _____. Henry has his

seatbelt on and he is _____ _____.

Both cars go to the side _____ _____ _____. A woman

_____ _____ _____ her car and says she is sorry. She says, "It is my

fault." No one _____ _____.

1. They call the _____.
2. They give each other their _____ numbers. (618-233-_____)
   and 618-377-_____)
3. They give each other their _____ information.
4. They give each other the _____ of their insurance companies.
5. They give each other information on their _____ registration papers.
6. Then they wait for the _____.

Basic Dictations © 2013 Catherine Sadow and Judy DeFilippo

The next day Henry calls his insurance company to report the accident.

Read the license plate numbers and the states they are from to your partner and have your partner repeat them to you.

Hawaii **MZA 275** ALOHA STATE	**NEW YORK** **FAC 9109** THE EMPIRE STATE	**Florida** **39 776** THE SUNSHINE STATE
Vermont **AAF 785** GREEN MOUNTAIN STATE	**Michigan** **AB 2545** GREAT LAKE STATE	**Massachusetts** **41E P00** THE SPIRIT OF AMERICA
Illinois **LMB 1** LAND OF LINCOLN	**Wisconsin** **15A 77V** America's Dairyland	**New Hampshire** **VS 37647** LIVE FREE OR DIE
California **260 295** EUREKA	**NEW JERSEY** **BCC 87** THE GARDEN STATE	**PUERTO RICO** **HET-749** Isla del Encanto

Discussion

1. Whose fault was the accident?
2. Have you ever been in a car accident? Tell your partner about it.

How to Get a Driver's License

Teacher's note:
CD track 57
Full text 147
Instuctions
for doing the
dictation:
page 116

Introduction

To get a driver's license in most states, you need to be 16 years old, learn the traffic laws of your state, and take several tests.

Vocabulary and Pronunciation

1. **Registry of Motor Vehicles (RMV)**: the department in charge of cars, driver's licenses, vehicle registrations.
2. **vehicles**: cars, bicycles, motorcycles, trucks, buses, etc.
3. **vision**: sight

NEW YORK STATE
DRIVER LICENSE

BARBARA J. FIALA
Comissioner
of Motor Vehicles
ID: 666 947 311

DOB: 02-16-90
TORRES, MARIA, J.
437 VALLEY RD
WEBSTER NY 14580
SEX: F EYES: BR HT:5-05
CLASS: D E:
ISSUED: 07-25-14
EXPIRES: 02-07-17

Prediction Dictation - Fill in the words you think are correct.

What should you do? First go to the Registry of Motor Vehicles _____ get a Driver's Handbook. Study the laws _____ the _____ . When you are ready to take the written _____ , go back to the RMV and take _____. If you pass the _____, you will get a learner's permit. You will also have a vision _____ and a road sign test.

If you _____ a new driver, you must practice a lot. There must always be a licensed driver _____ _____ car with _____. Some people go _____ driving schools. When you think _____ are ready for a road _____ , make an appointment to take _____. If you don't pass the _____ test, you can take _____ again. After you pass the _____ test, the Registry of Motor Vehicles will mail your license to _____.

 Basic Dictations © 2013 Catherine Sadow and Judy DeFilippo

Listening Dictation - Listen and fill in the blank spaces.

> What should you do? First go to the Registry of Motor Vehicles _____ get a Driver's Handbook. Study the laws _____ the _____ . When you are ready to take the written _____, go back to the RMV and take _____. If you pass the _____, you will get a learner's permit. You will also have a vision _____ and a road sign test.
>
> If you _____ a new driver, you must practice a lot. There must always be a licensed driver _____ _____ car with _____. Some people go _____ driving schools. When you think _____ are ready for a road _____, make an appointment to take _____. If you don't pass the _____ test, you can take _____ again. After you pass the _____ test, the Registry of Motor Vehicles will mail your license to _____.

Listening

Listen to the conversation and answer the following questions. Check your answers with a partner.

1. Why is Pat nervous?
2. Check the things she should bring with her to the Registry of Motor Vehicles.

____ $100.00
____ her glasses
____ a photo ID
____ $30.00
____ her birth certificate
____ something she has signed
____ something that shows where she lives

3. After Pat gets her learner's permit, what is she going to do?

Discussion

1. Can you drive?
2. Do you have a driver's license?
3. Is it difficult to get a driver's license in your country?
4. Was it difficult to get a driver's license here?

Road Signs

Teacher's note:
CD track 58
Full text 148
Instuctions
for doing the
dictation:
page 116

Introduction

You can see road signs at the side of roads to give information to drivers. We must pay attention to these signs so that we will not have any accidents. Some signs are now international. Pictures, not words, help travelers in different countries.

Vocabulary and Pronunciation - Talk about the meaning of each sign..

1. No trucks

2. Railroad crossing

3. 55 miles per hour

4. Highway route number

5. No U turn

6. No left turn

7. One way traffic

8. No exit

9. Police will remove your car

10. Pedestrian crossing

11. Intersection ahead

12. Drive slowly

13. Construction

14. Parking

15. Handicapped parking

16. Toll charge

Basic Dictations © 2013 Catherine Sadow and Judy DeFilippo

Dictogloss - Listen once, then write what you remember. With a partner, try to reconstruct the sentence.

1. _____

2. _____

3. _____

Listening

A Tic Tac Toe Bingo-type game

Here are 9 empty boxes. In the box below them there are 12 words for traffic/road signs. Choose one word to write in each box. You will use only nine boxes. Order is not important. When you are finished writing, your teacher is going to say the words in random order. As you listen, cross out the ones you wrote. The winner of the game is the first person to get three DOWN, three ACROSS, or three DIAGONALLY. Listen carefully to your teacher.

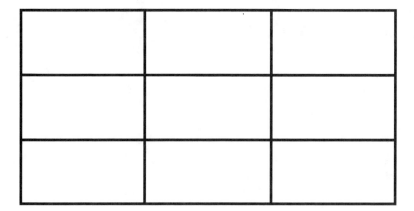

Choose the words to put in your boxes.

stop	one way	no trucks	hospital
left turn only	railroad	no passing zone	do not enter
dead end	speed limit 60	toll ahead $1.00	slow

Discussion 1

Talk about the meanings of these signs.

1.

2.

3.

4.

5.

6.

7.

8.

Discussion 2

1. Most U.S. highways have speed limits of between 60 and 70 miles per hour. What speed limits, if any, do you have in your country?

2. If you don't stop at a stop sign and the police see you, you have to pay a fine. Do you have to pay fines in your country if you do not pay attention to road signs? What if you go through a red light?

Full Dictation Texts

There are four types of dictation used in this book. Here are instructions on how to do them. The introduction gives other suggestions.

1. Partial (sometimes known as *cloze*)

Most of the dictations in this text are partial dictations where words, phrases, or chunks of language have been deleted, and students are required to listen and write down the missing words. All the dictations should be discussed upon completion. Pair work is encouraged, and spelling can be corrected at the time of completion.

2. Pair (sometimes known as *mutual*)

This dictation requires students to work in pairs to combine two partial texts into one continuous piece. One student (Student A) has a gapped copy of the dictation, and the other student (Student B) has a different gapped copy. Each student has half of the text. They should not look at each other's texts. Student A dictates and Student B writes, then B dictates and A writes, back and forth, and so on until the story is complete. The first one the students do should be modeled first.

3. Dictogloss

In this kind of dictation, the focus is on getting the gist or main idea of a sentence. Students are told that they will hear a sentence only once after which they are to jot down the words they can recall and try to reconstruct the sentence in writing as accurately as they can. The first time this is done, the teacher will probably have to allow the students a second reading until they discover that they need to pay attention the first time around. This is especially true for beginning level students. As the students work at rebuilding the sentences, they can work in pairs or groups of three or four. Some teachers like to have students write their sentences on the board for all to see, correct, and discuss.

4. Prediction

Prediction lessons come in two parts. The first part focuses more on reading skills and grammar. The students can work individually or in pairs, reading the passage and predicting (or guessing) what should be in each blank space. Any logical or grammatically correct word or phrase can be accepted. The second part requires the students to listen to the same passage and see if their guesses were correct, or similar.

Friends and Families

What Is Your Name?
Partial dictation   page 1   CD Track 1

Hello. My **name** is Ji Young. I **am** from South Korea. In my English **class** there are students from different countries. Ken **is** from Japan, Rosa is **from** Mexico. Ahmed and Khalid **are** from Iraq. Ozzie **is** from Turkey. We are **a** small class. **We** are friends.

What's Your Nickname?
Partial dictation   page 2   CD Track 2

Hi! My name **is** Elizabeth June Gomez. At school, I **am** Elizabeth. At home, **my** name is Liz. With my **friends**, I am EJ. With my **soccer** coach, I am Gomez. At **work** I am Beth. I am a girl **with** many names!

The Garcia Family
Partial dictation   page 3   CD Track 3

The Garcia family **is from** San Diego, California. Joe and Anna **are** married. Joe is **Anna's** husband. Anna is Joe's wife. Joe **and** Anna are parents **of two** children, Tom and Lisa. Tom is **their** son, and Lisa **is** their daughter. Anna is Lisa and Tom's **mother**. Joe is Lisa and Tom's **father**. Joe and Anna are U.S. citizens **now**. They came **from** Mexico in 2001.

The Jolie-Pitt Family
Partial dictation   page 4   CD Track 4

Angelina Jolie is a famous **American** actress, writer, **and** director. She is also famous **because of** her humanitarian work **with** third world countries. She and **her** partner, actor Brad Pitt, have **six** children. Three are adopted: Maddox (born in **2001**) is from Cambodia, Pax (2003) **is from** Vietnam, and Zahara (**2005**) is from Ethiopia. Brad and Angelina have three biological **children**: a daughter, Shiloh (2006), and **twins** Knox and Vivienne, born **in 2008**.

Ted's Family

Partial dictation   page 5   CD Track 5

_____ 1. Ted Johnson is **26 years old**. (yes)

_____ 2. His **brother's** name is Jim. (yes)

_____ 3. His brother Jim **is married to** Susan. (no)

_____ 4. Ted's **mother** is 58 years old. (no)

_____ 5. Ted's **sister-in-law** is Amy. (yes)

_____ 6. Ted's **parents** are Mike and Lisa. (yes)

_____ 7. Ted has **two grandfathers**. (yes)

_____ 8. Jenna is Ted's **nephew**. (no)

_____ 9. Ted's **father**, Mike, has a **brother**, Bob. (yes)

_____10. Is Jay Ted's **uncle**? (no)

_____ 11. Is Lisa **Ted's mother**? (yes)

_____ 12. Lisa and Lee **are sisters**. (yes)

_____ 13. Ted has **two aunts**. (no)

_____ 14. Jenna and Jay **are cousins**. (yes)

_____ 15. Ted's **grandmothers** are Lisa and Amy. (no)

My New Family

Partial dictation   page 7   CD Track 6

I am **65** years old. My first wife is dead. Now I am married to a widow, and **I love her** very much. We are **very happy**. She **has** one daughter and **two** grandchildren, a **boy** and a **girl**. They are **8** and **10** years old. There is a problem. When we go to their house or eat at a restaurant I try **to talk** to the two grandchildren. But **they are** playing games on their iPhones all **the time**. All I get are **one-word** answers. I think this is **very** rude.

I think **it is** wrong. I want **to say** something about this, but my wife doesn't want me **to talk** to her daughter **or** son-in-law or to the children **about this**. She says that this is the way it is now. Times are changing. **Next week** we are going to be **going out** again with them. I don't want **to go**. What should **I do**?

Harry

Man's Best Friend

Pair dictation   pages 8-9   CD Track 7

1. 40% of U.S. homes have a pet dog.
2. 43% cook special food for their dogs.
3. 79% of Americans give their pets Christmas or birthday gifts.
4. 33% talk to their pets on the phone.
5. 84% call themselves the dog's "mother" or "father".

Listening

Harry: Dad, can I have a puppy?

Dad: I don't think so, Harry. We are so busy that we don't have time to take care of a dog.

Harry: I don't think it's so much work.

Dad: Well, Harry, someone has to take the dog out many times until it learns not to go to the bathroom in the house.

Harry: I can do that.

Dad: When the dog is older, someone has to take the dog out three times a day in the rain or snow for as long as we have the dog. Can you take the dog out before you go to school?

Harry: But I have to be at school at eight o'clock. What else do I have to do?

Dad: You have to be sure that there is always water in the dog's water bowl and give it the correct dog food. Sometimes you'll have to take it to the vet. Also you have to train the dog.

Harry: Dad, I still want a puppy. Can I have one?

Dad: I'll think about it.

Answers: Numbers 1, 4, 5, 7, 10

Let's Talk

Partial dictation page 10 CD Track 8

Dear Friend,

   I **want** our family **to talk** to each other more, but **it is** very difficult. We are **four** people, my husband and I and a teenage **son** and a teenage daughter. Everyone in our **house** has a cell phone, and we also have **four** television sets and four computers. At breakfast **we don't talk**. My children and my husband **are eating** their breakfast and checking their **cell phones**. At night my **son** goes to his **room** to do his homework and **play** videogames on his **computer**. My daughter **goes to her room** to do her homework and **text** to her friends on her phone. My husband goes to the living room to **watch** news and baseball. I feel very alone. No one in our family talks. What **can I do**?

   Sad Mother

Am I Too Old? Asking for Advice

Pair dictation pages 11-12 CD Track 9

Dear Friend,

   I am 71 years old. I am a widow. I retired from my job as a nurse five years ago. I have two sons but they live in different cities.

   My sons don't want me to drive. They say I am too old. If I don't drive, I will have to stay home a lot. What should I do?

   Young Grandma

Match Answers

Her sons think (g) she is too old to drive.   She doesn't want (f) to stay home.
They don't want her (c) to drive.   She was (d) a nurse.
She is (e) a widow.   She has (a) two sons.
Five years ago (b) she retired.

Dictogloss

1. I don't want to stay home.
2. Is 16 too young to drive?
3. Is 71 very old?

Who is Important?

| Partial dictation | page 13 | CD Track 10 |

> **Introduction: notes to teacher**
> Students' answers will vary but a few suggestions are:
> 1. rich people: Bill Gates, Oprah Winfrey, Madonna, Queen Elizabeth
> 2. Nobel Peace Prize winners: Barack Obama, Nelson Mandela, Kofi Annan
> 3. Academy Award winners, male or female: Meryl Streep, Tom Hanks, Sean Penn

1. Name **a few teachers** who **helped** you in school or college.
2. Name three friends who have helped you through a **difficult time**.
3. Think of three people you enjoy **spending time with**.
4. **Think of** a few people whom **you love**.

Numbers

Using Numbers

| Partial dictation | page 14 | CD Track 11 |

1. My telephone number is **212-453-8976**.
2. His address is **6848** Washington Street.
3. Her zip code is **02034**.
4. Her I.D. number is **976-661-30100**.
5. His email address is **jbfitz88@aol.com**.

More With Numbers

| Pair dictation | page 15 | CD Track 12 |

SEPTEMBER						
SUN	MON	TUES	WED	THURS	FRI	SAT
		1	2 Full Moon	3	4	5 *family party* *3:00*
dinner with 6 *the Smiths* *at 5*	7 Labor Day	8	*first day* 9 *of class*	10	11	*baseball* 12 *game*
birthday 13 *party*	14	*dentist* 15 *2:00*	16	17	18	19
20	21	*hair* 22 *4:00*	*birthday* 23 *party*	24	25	26
27	28	*doctor's* 29 *appointment*	*birthday* 3:00 30 Blue Moon			

American Money

Partial dictation page 17 CD Track 13

1. Jen has two **pennies**, three dimes, **one** nickel, two quarters, **and** a five-**dollar bill**. How much money **is this**? ($5.87)

2. Ben is buying a hat. It's **$15.00**. He has a twenty-dollar **bill**. How much **is** his change? ($5.00)

3. A shoe store is having **a** sale. Bob **is buying** two pairs of sneakers at **$26.00** each. How much money **is that**? ($52.00)

4. The **five** members of the Baxter family **are** in a restaurant eating dinner. Each dinner is $15.50. How much is the **bill**? ($77.50)

A Little Math • Add and Subtract

Partial dictation page 18 CD Track 14

1. Draw **three** lines in a row. Write **20** on the first **line**. Write **30** on the last line. Add the two numbers together. **Write** your answer **on the** middle line.

    20 50 30
  ——— ——— ———

2. Draw **five** lines in a row. Write **100** on the **first** line. Write **20** on the second **line**. Subtract the smaller number **from** the bigger number. **Write** your answer on the middle **line**.

    100 20 80
  ——— ——— ——— ——— ———

3. Draw a circle. Write **45** above the **circle**. Write **5** below the circle. Subtract the **smaller** number from the **bigger** number. Write **the** answer inside the circle.

4. **Draw** a triangle. **Write 90** over the triangle. Write **10** under the triangle. Add the numbers together and write the answer inside the **triangle**.

5. **Draw** a circle. **Draw** a triangle under the circle. Put **42** in the circle. Put **48** in the triangle. **Add** the numbers together. Put your answer below the triangle.

Fun With Numbers

Partial dictation   page 20   CD Track 15

1. Draw **five** lines in a row. Write **5** on the second **line**. Write **10** on the first line. Multiply the **two numbers** and put the answer **on the last** line.

   <u>   10   </u> <u>   5   </u> <u>   </u> <u>   </u> <u>   50   </u>

2. Draw a circle. Above the **circle**, write **16**. Below the circle, write **2**.
   Divide the **bigger** number by the smaller number. Put the answer in the circle.

   16
   ⑧
   2

3. Draw **four** lines **in a row**. Write the number **6** on the first **line** and the number **2** on the second line. Multiply the two numbers and put your answer **on the last line**.

   <u>   6   </u> <u>   2   </u> <u>   </u> <u>   12   </u>

Dictogloss   page 21

1. Five times five is twenty-five.
2. Seventeen and three is twenty.

Listening

In almost every culture there are lucky and unlucky numbers. In the Far East, in countries like Japan, three is a very lucky number because it is like the word for living or life. But also in the Far East, four is a very unlucky number because it is like the word for death or dying.

In Western countries like the United States seven is a very lucky number. On July 7, 2007, many people got married because it was a very lucky day for getting married. A very unlucky number in Western countries is thirteen. In some buildings there are a twelfth floor and a fourteenth floor, but no thirteenth floor.

Answers			
	3	lucky	East
	4	unlucky	East
	7	lucky	West
	13	unlucky	West

Trivia Contest

    Partial dictation   page 22   CD Track 16

1. **On what date** do Americans celebrate Valentine's Day? (Feb. 14th)
2. What does **9/11** stand for? (Attack in NYC / World Trade Center (2001))
3. What percent is **a good tip** in a restaurant? (15% to 20%)
4. **How much is** a pack of cigarettes? (local price–check it!)
5. What is the average yearly salary of a **public school teacher**?
    ($65,000 – $72,000 – 2012 figures)
6. How much sleep **do most people** need each night? (7 to 9 hours)
7. **How many children** do Angelina Jolie and Brad Pitt have? (Six, three adopted)
8. What is the average total time a commuter travels **to and from** work? (50 min.)
9. What is **the normal body** temperature in Fahrenheit? (98.6 degrees)
10. **What number** do many Americans think is unlucky? (Number 13)

    Answers to discussion on Trivia Page
    Accept all answers, even the seemingly outrageous ones!

Time

What Time Is It? Part 1

    Partial dictation   page 23   CD Track 17

1. The Higgins Hospital Visiting Hours are from **3:00** P.M. to **8:00** P.M.

2. The South School is open from **7:00** A.M. to **4:00** P.M.

3. The car repair shop business hours are **8:00** A.M. to **5:00** P.M.

4. The store hours for Bob's Bookstore are
    Sundays **12:00 to 6:00**
    Monday through Saturday **9:00 to 9:00**.

5. The hours for Terry's Restaurant are
    Lunch: **11:00** A.M. to **3:00** P.M.
    Dinner: **5:00** P.M. to **10:00** P.M.

6. The North River Medical Center's hours are
    Monday through Friday, **8:00** A.M. to **8:00** P.M.
    Weekends, emergencies only, **7:00** A.M. to **7:00** P.M.

What Time Is It? Part 2

Partial dictation   page 25   CD Track 18

Introduction Note to teachers: when saying the time, say: six-thirty, eight fifteen, etc.

Milton Bus Company Tickets
One way **$12.00**
Round trip **$18.00**

Milton to Newton		Newton to Milton	
Leaves Milton	Arrives Newton	Leaves Newton	Arrives Milton
6:30 A.M.	**8:15 A.M.**	**7:00 A.M.**	**8:45 A.M.**
11:15 A.M.	**1:00 P.M.**	**2:15 P.M.**	**4:00 P.M.**
6:45 P.M.	**8:30 P.M.**	**7:30 P.M.**	**9:15 P.M.**

The Days of the Week

Partial dictation   page 28   CD Track 19

1. What days **are you** in English class?
2. What day **is** before **Saturday**?
3. What day **is** after **Monday**?
4. What **two days** are the weekend days?
5. **What days** do most people go to **work**?
6. How many days **are** in one **week**?

The Months of the Year

Partial dictation   page 30   CD Track 20

Dictation 1 (Say the date. *For example*: January 20th , 2015; then leave time for the students to write 1/20/2015)

1. May 1, 2012   (5/1/12)
2. February 14, 2001   (2/14/01)
3. June 7, 1976   (6/7/76)
4. April 1, 2011   (4/1/11)
5. November 25, 2013 (11/25/13)

Dictation 2 (Leave time for the students to circle the correct answer.)

1. Is January **the first month**? (a. Yes, it is)
2. When is **your birthday**? (a. in March)
3. **How many days** does May have? (b. 31)
4. When does the **school year begin**? (a. In September)

The Four Seasons

Dictogloss   page 31   CD Track 21

1. Winter is cold with snow and ice.
2. Spring is warm with sun and rain.
3. Summer is sunny and hot.
4. Fall is the cool time of year.

What's the Weather? The Temperature?

Partial dictation   page 32   CD Track 22

Good morning! I'm Bob Walker with the weather for today, March 28th. It's a cold snowy day in New York. Temperatures in the 20s, all day.

In Chicago, it's a cloudy day, but cold, with temperatures only in the teens.

In the South it's warmer. Miami is sunny and hot with temperatures around 80 today.

In Houston, Texas, it's windy and cool, around 55 degrees. Maybe a little sun in the afternoon.

On the West Coast it's partly cloudy in Los Angeles with warm temperatures in the 60s, and in Seattle, it's also partly cloudy in the 50s. Maybe some rain tonight.

City	Weather	Temperatures
New York	cold, snowy	20s
Chicago	cloudy, cold	teens
Miami	sunny, hot	80s
Houston	windy, cool	50s
Los Angeles	partly cloudy, warm	60s
Seattle	partly cloudy, maybe rain	50s

U.S. Holidays and Special Days

Partial dictation   page 35   CD Track 23

1. Name the **two** famous American presidents **with** February birthdays. (Washington & Lincoln)
2. Name **the month** when the U.S. celebrates **its birthday**. (July)
3. Are there any **holidays in August**? (no)
4. What two holidays **are in November**? (Veterans' Day & Thanksgiving)
5. What special **day is for** lovers? (Feb. 14, Valentine's Day)
6. What two holidays do **children love**? (Halloween and Christmas)

Around Town

Let's Go Shopping

Pair dictations   pages 37-38   CD Track 24

How much is this coat on sale?

It's $20.00.

What is the regular price of the coat?

It's $30.00. You save $10.00!

That's a good price!

Yes, and today you can buy it for $15.00.

That's great. I'll take it.

Cash or charge?

Cash.

Second-Hand Clothing Stores

Partial dictation   page 39   CD Track 25

This is Sam. He **is** from San Francisco. He is **my** classmate. He goes shopping at **the** Goodwill Store. He can save **money** because the clothes there **are** second hand. That means his clothes **are** used. At the Goodwill **store** he can buy a warm winter jacket **for** $25.   That's **a** good price. The **jacket** is clean and comfortable. Today **he** is wearing black **shoes** from the Salvation Army Store. They **are** new, not used! The price tag is still on them. The price **is** only $15!

Household Items

Prediction dictation   pages 42   CD Track 26

Hi. My name **is** Chen. I am 23 years **old**. I am from Beijing, China, and I **live** with my family in Chinatown **in** San Francisco.   Our **apartment** building has four floors. Our apartment is on the second **floor**. It's comfortable. There **are** a kitchen, a **living** room, two bedrooms, and **one** bathroom. I share a **bedroom** with my two brothers. My brothers and I **are** students. My parents work **at** a small grocery **store** nearby. I love my **family** a lot. We are happy here **in the** United States.

Used Furnishings

Pair dictations   pages 43-44   CD Track 27

I'm calling about your sewing machine.
Yes. It's a Singer Model 327.
What condition is it in?
Well, it needs repair. It's a 1990.
How much would it cost to fix it?
Probably about $50. I'm not sure.
Thank you.

Looking for an Apartment

Dictogloss   page 46   CD Track 28

1. I'm calling about your apartment for rent.
2. How much is the rent per month?
3. When is the apartment available?
4. Is there a laundry room?

Sending Money Home by Western Union

Partial dictation   page 47   CD Track 29

Mr. and Mrs. Gonzales **go to the** information counter at the supermarket. They **tell** the clerk that they **want to** send money using Western Union. They give the clerk **$500** and a fee for "Next Day" service. Mr. Gonzales **tells the clerk** his name and address and his mother's **name**. Then he gives the clerk the **address** of a Western Union store or office **near her house**. He also **gets** a 10-digit money transfer control number (MTCN). After he has done this, **he calls his mother** in Bogota and tells her the number. Next **day** his mother goes to the store with a Western Union in it. She **shows** the clerk her ID and tells him the 10-digit number. He **gives her the money** in cash.

Listening   page 48

Mother: Hello…
Charlie: Hi, Mom, how are you?
Mother: Hi, Charlie. Is everything OK? I just spoke to you yesterday.
Charlie: I have a problem. Something is wrong with my car and I don't have enough money to fix it. But I need my car to go to work.
Mother: How much money do you need?

Charlie: $800.

Mother: Oh my. Yes, I can send it to you. How soon do you need it?

Charlie: Tomorrow.

Mother: I can send it by Western Union. We're both in the States so I can send it Home Delivery.

Charlie: Thank you, Mom. I'll pay you back at the end of the month when I am paid.

Answers

1. The son, Charlie.
2. His mother.
3. He needs $800.
4. He needs to fix his car.
5. She will send him $800. She will do it immediately.
6. She will send it by Western Union "Home Delivery."
7. He will send her the money at the end of the month when he receives his pay check.

United States Postal Service

Pair dictations   pages 50-51   CD Track 30

1. Almost every town has a post office.
2. In small towns we often get our mail at the post office.
3. In our town our mail carrier brings mail to us.
4. Free delivery of mail began in 1836 in the cities.
5. In the countryside it began in 1896.

Listening   page 52

Post Office Clerk: Good morning. What can I do for you today?

Customer: I need to mail this parcel.

Post Office Clerk: How do you want to mail it?

Customer: What do you mean?

Post Office Clerk: How fast do you want it to get there?

Customer: Sometime this week.

Post Office Clerk: We can send it Priority Mail. It will get there in three days.

Customer: That's good.

Post Office Clerk: That will be $14.72.

Customer: Here you are.

Post Office Clerk: Do you need any stamps?

Customer: No, I don't, thank you.

Answers   1, 2, 3, 7, 8

Public Schools in the United States

Partial dictation   page 53   CD Track 31

Dictation 1

This is a story about the Jones family. Bob and Susan Jones have four children. Their son John is 5 years old. He's in kindergarten at the Center Elementary School. Their daughter Sara is seven years old. She's in the second grade at the Center Elementary School. Their son Ben is twelve years old. He's in the sixth grade at the North Middle School. Their daughter Jenny is 16 years old. She's in the 10th grade at West High School.

	Age	Grade	School
John	5	Kindergarten	Center Elementary
Sara	7	second	Center Elementary
Ben	12	6th	North Middle
Jenny	16	10th	West High School

Dictation 2

1. What grade **is Ben in**?   (b. The 6th grade.)
2. Is Sara **eight years old**?   (a. No, she's seven.)
3. How many children are in the **elementary school**?   (c. two)

In the Library

Dictogloss   page 55   CD Track 32

1. A library card is free for everyone.
2. My mother is a member of a book club.
3. With my card I can take home movies.

Listening   page 55

A. Excuse me. I want to get a library card.
B. Do you live here in town?
A. Yes, I do.
B. Good. To get a card you need two pieces of identification. One can be a driver's license or a student photo ID. The other can be a letter with your name and address on it to show that you live in this town. You can also show us a utility bill with your address on it.
A. Thank you.

Keep America Beautiful

Partial dictation   page 56   CD Track 33

Dictation

Do you sometimes **toss** a cigarette butt or a piece of **paper**, like a candy wrapper on the ground? Cigarette butts are the most littered things **in the** world. Over four trillion cigarette butts are littered **in the** world **in a year**. They last **for a long time**. Most of us like a clean place **to live in**, so why do we litter?

Dictogloss

1. Don't toss things on the ground.
2. Recycle newspapers and paper cups.

Listening   page 57

What are some things that we throw away that we can recycle? We throw away plastic containers, soda cans, and cigarette butts. We throw away lots of paper, such as candy wrappers and newspapers.

We also throw away some big things that are very bad for the environment, like tires and old cars. All of this causes pollution, and the pollution goes into our water, our air, and the ground. We need to put more things into our recycle containers and our rubbish bins so that our world will be less polluted.

Answers   3, 4, 6, 8, 9, 10, 13

Food

Fruit Salad

Partial dictation   page 58   CD Track 34

The class **is going to** have a party. Some students **are making** cookies. Some students **are** bringing soft drinks. The teacher **is bringing** coffee and **tea**. One student **is making** a **fruit salad**. She is putting strawberries, **bananas**, pears, **and apples** in **the fruit salad**. **It will be** delicious.

Listening   page 59

Man: What are you making for the class party?
Woman: I'm making a large fruit salad.
Man: What are you putting in the fruit salad?
Woman: I'm putting in grapes, bananas, apples, and strawberries.
Man: You know, pears are on sale at the supermarket this week.
Woman: Great! I'll get four or five pears and put them in the fruit salad.

Answers

1. She is making a fruit salad to bring to the school party,
2. She is putting in grapes, bananas, apples, strawberries, and pears.
3. Pears are on sale at the supermarket.

A Supermarket List

Partial dictation   page 60   CD Track 35

Mrs. Smith is **too busy** with their **new baby** to go to the supermarket. She **gives** Mr. Smith a list of things **she needs**. She tells him, "**These** are the important things. Please **don't forget** the diapers. We **have only** three **or four**. We also **need** toilet paper. We have only one roll left. We need **coffee,** and I need **tomato** sauce. **We need** everything on the list."

She also gives him her supermarket card and **some** coupons so he can **get** a lot of things **on sale**. Mr. Smith **takes** the list and asks, " Is there anything else **you need**?" Mrs. Smith says, "I'll **call you** on your cell phone if I think of something."

Listening   page 61

Mrs. Smith: I'm too busy to go to the supermarket.

Mr. Smith: I can go. Give me a list of what you need.

Mrs. Smith: Okay. I have coupons so I know the prices.

Mr. Smith: Okay

Mrs. Smith: Please get me two boxes of diapers. They will cost $18.00. I also want four cans of tuna fish. They are on sale for $5.00 and three cans of tomato sauce for $1.00.

Mr. Smith: That must be on sale also. Is that all?

Mrs. Smith: No, we also need one can of coffee. It's on sale for $3.49, and we need toilet paper. Twelve rolls will cost $6.99, and also paper towels. Eight rolls are on sale for $5.00.

Mr. Smith: Anything else?

Mrs. Smith: Please buy two boxes of cereal on sale for $5.00 and one and a half pounds of red grapes for $2.69. Make sure they're fresh.

Answers a. 2 boxes diapers $18.00   e. 12 rolls toilet paper $6.99
b. 4 cans tuna fish $5.00   f. 8 rolls paper towels $5.00
c. 3 cans tomato sauce $1.00   g. 2 boxes cereal $5.00
d. 1 can coffee $3.49   h. 1.5 lbs. red grapes $2.69
(Total cost is about $50.00)

Nothing to Eat!

Partial dictation   page 63   CD Track 36

Dear Friend,

Help! There is nothing **good to eat** in my house. Our refrigerator **is empty**. Why? Because my mother, my sister, **and my grandmother** are all on diets. I AM NOT on a diet, and I **am starving**! I like steak and hamburgers, **potatoes**, and **rice**. I want an ice cream or **a pizza** when I come home **from school**. My mother is eating only **salads** and **fish**. My sister **is eating** lots of vegetables and fruits. My grandmother is eating **lots of** chicken. We never **eat out**. I am going crazy! What **can I do**?

Starving Steven, 17

Eat Right!

Partial dictation   page 64   CD Track 37

1. It's important to **eat three meals a day**. (agree)
2. It's important to have foods from **the five food groups** each day. (agree)
3. A hamburger with French fries is **a healthy dinner**. (disagree)
4. Bananas, **pears**, and cherries are examples of **the fruit group**. (agree)
5. Cheese, milk, and **bread** are examples of the **meat** group. (disagree)
6. A healthy dinner would be fish, vegetables, **rice**, **and fruit**. (agree)

Food Pantries

Prediction dictation   page 66   CD Track 38

How does a food pantry work? There is **a** large place where many companies donate food that **is** good, and that they cannot sell. There are farmers who may have extra cucumbers or **extra** potatoes or **extra** onions. There are food manufacturers that may have **extra** cans **of soup** that they didn't sell. There are big supermarkets that may have **extra** food that they did not **sell** because they bought too much.

Many restaurants donate **food** that they did not use and which may spoil in a few **days**. Schools, churches, and community centers ask people to **donate** food. They will collect it **and** bring it to the food **pantry**. Sometimes they ask people to bring **foods** that are healthy, like peanut butter or tuna fish.

People who need **food** can shop at **the** food pantry when **it is** open and there are volunteers there to serve them. And the food is **free**.

Listening (Two friends are talking.)   page 66

Martha: What are you doing tomorrow? Let's get together.

Linda: Sorry. I volunteer at the food pantry every Friday.

Martha: Really? What do you do there?

Linda: I sort the food that has come in. I put the potatoes with the vegetables and the new cans of soup with the other soups.

Martha: What kinds of foods did you have last week?

Linda: There were two kinds of pasta. There was also pasta sauce. There were bags of rice and also bags of noodles. There were carrots. There were some cans of tuna fish. There were a few jars of peanut butter. That's very popular. There were also lots of onions. One of the supermarkets gave us jars of strawberry jam. We also had some white bread and some wheat bread.

Martha: Did many people come?

Linda: Oh, yes. When we opened at 10:00 in the morning, there were many people waiting.

Martha: You are doing good volunteer work.

Linda: Yes, and I really enjoy doing it.

Answers to the Listening

potatoes, cans of soup, pasta, pasta sauce, rice, noodles. carrots, cans of tuna fish, jars of peanut butter, onions, jars of strawberry jam, white bread, wheat bread

Tipping

Prediction dictation   page 68   CD Track 39

Peter is having dinner with **his** wife **in a** nice restaurant. After **he** finishes his coffee, the waiter gives him his check. It **is** exactly $60.00 and that includes the state tax. Peter adds 15% of $60.00 to the bill. It **is** $9.00. He wants **to** give the **waiter** $69.00. His **wife** says, "He is a good waiter. Give **him** 20%." Peter changes the amount to **20%**. It **is** $12.00. He gives the **waiter** **$72.00**. The **waiter** says, "**Thank you**."

Answers for What is the Amount?

Amount	15%	Total	*or*	Amount	20%	Total
$10.00	$1.50	$11.50		$10.00	$2.00	$12.00
$20.00	$3.00	$23.00		$20.00	$4.00	$24.00
$30.00	$4.50	$34.50		$30.00	$6.00	$36.00
$40.00	$6.00	$46.00		$40.00	$8.00	$48.00
$90.00	$13.50	$103.50		$90.00	$18.00	$108.00

Listening   page 68

Carlos: I never know who to tip in the United States or how much to tip. For example, do I tip a taxi driver?

Joe: Yes, you should tip the taxi driver. Fifteen percent.

Carlos: I didn't know that. I never tip the taxi driver when I go to the airport.

Joe: You don't have to tip the guy who puts gas in your car.

Carlos: Really? Sometimes I give him a dollar.

Joe: You don't have to.

Carlos: What about my mail carrier?

Joe: Don't tip him. If you want to, you can give him a present at Christmas.

Carlos: Do I need to tip my barber when I get a haircut?

Joe: Definitely. Barbers and hairdressers always get tips.

Carlos: So, when I go to the coffee shop or ice cream store, there's a tip jar. What should I do?

Joe: You don't have to put anything in it. But if my ice cream costs $2.50 and I give the person who's serving me $3.00, I put the change into the tip jar.

Carlos: Well, thanks for the help.

Joe: That's OK, and next time remember to tip the cab driver.

Answers to Listening   taxi driver, barber, hairdresser

Health

A Bad Morning

Partial dictation   page 69   CD Track 40

When Henry wakes up **Monday** morning, his **head, ears**, and **throat** hurt. He also **has** a bad backache. He tells **his wife** that he has **to go** to work.

His wife takes his temperature. She says, "You are not going **to work today**. You have a fever of 102 degrees.

"I am going **to give** you **some** aspirin, some Vitamin C, and some **hot** chicken soup. If you **feel bad** tomorrow, we **are going** to the doctor. I think **you have** the flu."

Listening   page 70

Wife: Henry, What's the matter? You look sick.

Henry: I feel bad. I have a very bad headache. I have a sore throat, and my ears ache. Also my back hurts. But I've got to go to work. It's very important.

Wife: You are NOT going to go to work. I'm going to take your temperature.

Henry: OK. ....What is it?

Wife: It's 102 degrees, Henry. Go back to bed. I'm going to bring you aspirin, Vitamin C, and hot chicken soup.

Answers Numbers 3, 5, and 8 are not in the listening script.

An Appointment for Henry

Partial dictation   page 71   CD Track 41

Secretary: Hello. This is Dr. Cutler's office. **Please** hold for a minute. I'll be right with you........   Good morning. Can I help you?

Wife: Good morning. This is Ellen Magill. I need an appointment **for my husband**, Henry.

Secretary: Is this for a check up? The next appointment **we have** is next month, **April ten**.

Wife: **No**, **my husband** is sick now.

Secretary: If **this is** an emergency, he should go to the emergency **room** at the hospital.

Wife: I don't think so. His temperature has been 102 (degrees) for **three days**. I have given him **aspirin** every **four hours** but **it is** still 102.

Secretary: **I have** a cancellation at 2:30 (two thirty) this afternoon. Can **you be here** at 2:30?

Wife: We **will be there**. Thank you.

True or False   False, True, False, False, True

Henry Visits the Doctor

Partial dictation page 73 CD Track 42

First the doctor's assistant **takes** Henry's temperature, **and** it **is 102** degrees. She **takes** Henry's blood pressure, and **it is** a little high. She takes some blood from Henry, and she **asks him** to give her some urine. The blood and the urine **will** go to a lab,

Then Dr. Cutler **comes in**. He asks Henry **many** questions. He listens to Henry's **heart** and **lungs** with his stethoscope. He says to Henry, "I think **you have** the flu. I want you **to take this** to the pharmacy. This is a prescription **for some** medicine. Take it **three times a day** with meals. Drink **a lot of water**. Get **a lot of** rest. If you **are not better** by Friday, **call me**.

Listening

Doctor: Hello, Henry. How are you feeling?

Henry: Terrible. I feel terrible.

Doctor: Since when?

Henry: Since Monday. Three days.

Doctor: How old are you, Henry?

Henry: I'm 45.

Doctor: Your temperature is 102 degrees, and your blood pressure is a little high. I want to listen to your heart and lungs with my stethoscope.

Henry: Is everything OK?

Doctor: Your heart is OK, but your lungs don't sound good. I think you have the flu.

Henry: Is it serious?

Doctor: No. I will give you a prescription for some medicine. Go to the pharmacy and get the medicine. Take it three times a day. You will feel better by Friday or Saturday.

Answers 102 degrees, a little high, stethoscope, prescription, terrible, 45, pharmacy

Your Medical History

Partial dictation   page 76   CD Track 43

1. You have a headache, a **fever**, and a **cold**.
   You have: (b. the flu)

2. Flowers, animals, **and** dust make you **sneeze**.
   You have: (a. an allergy)

3. You are a heavy **smoker**. You started smoking when you were twelve.
   You may have: (a. lung cancer)

4. **You have** a temperature of 102 °.
   You have: (c. a fever)

5. You throw up **your food**.
   You have: (a. an upset stomach)

A Visit to the Dentist

Partial dictation   page 78   CD Track 44

Jack went **to the dentist** yesterday. He goes every **six months. First** the dental hygienist cleans **his teeth** and takes a few x-rays. Then the **dentist**, Dr. Fitch, looks in **his mouth** and says, "**You have** a cavity. I'm going to fill it now." She gives him some Novocain and fills **his cavity**.

The dental hygienist gives Jack **a new toothbrush**, a tube of **toothpaste**, and some dental floss. She says, "**Come back in six months**."

Dictogloss   page 79

1. Brush and floss every day.
2. Don't eat a lot of candy.

Listening   page 79

Jack: Hello. This is Jack Black. I'd like to make an appointment.
Secretary: When do you want to come?
Jack: Next Monday, March 19th.
Secretary: I'm sorry. The dentist is very busy on Monday. Can you come on
               Tuesday, March 20th at 4:30?
Jack: Yes, I can. Thank you.
Secretary: Goodbye, Jack. We'll see you on Tuesday.

Answers 4, 1, 7, 3, 2, 6, 5, 8

Baby Teeth

Pair dictation   pages 80-81   CD Track 45

Babies start to get teeth at nine or ten months old. Dentists say that it is very important to brush your baby's teeth two times a day. Use just a little bit of toothpaste. Babies won't like it, but it is important to do this.

Listening

Grandmother: Why is the baby crying?

Mother: He's crying because he doesn't like me to brush his teeth. He doesn't like the toothbrush or the toothpaste.

Grandmother: Why are you brushing his teeth? I never brushed your teeth when you were a baby.

Mother: That's why I have so many cavities and toothaches. Dentists say it is important to brush your baby's teeth.

Answers   Sentences 1, 3, and 4

Sleep Like a Baby

Pair dictation   pages 82-83   CD Track 46

Doctors say that we should get seven to nine hours of sleep every night. This is how to get a good night's sleep:

1. Don't go to bed if you are hungry. Eat a light snack.
2. Don't drink alcohol or coffee for four hours before going to sleep.
3. Put on warm socks.
4. Don't watch television in your bedroom just before going to sleep.
   Match the ages   d, f, c, b, e, a

Infant Immunizations

Dictogloss   page 84   CD Track 47

1. Take your baby to the doctor.
2. Babies cry when they get shots.

Partial dictation   page 85

In many states **children** must have some vaccinations **before** they can go **to school**. This is a law. The vaccines protect **them** from getting communicable diseases. Communicable means that **if one person** has a disease, many others **may get it** from that person.

For example, seventy **years** ago many children **had** polio and **some** children died. Everyone **was** afraid **of it**. Now, because there is a polio **vaccine**, polio is almost gone **from the United States**.

Work

How Much Do They Make?

Partial dictation pages 87-88 CD Track 48

Dictation, Part 1

1. I am a **mechanic**. My annual salary is **$50,000**.
2. She is a **doctor**. Her average salary is **$160,000**.
3. I am a **hair** stylist. I receive about **$40,000** a year.
4. The average **annual** salary of a pilot is **$150,000**.
5. Most **police officers** make an annual salary of about **$68,000**.

Dictation, Part 2 page 88

1. A pilot's average **salary** is **more** than a teacher's. (T)
2. A **plumber's** annual salary **is about** $65,000 a year.(F)
3. A **policeman** and a **teacher** make about the same. (T)
4. A **rock star's** salary is **more than** $200,000 a year. (T)
5. A doctor makes the same **annual salary** as a **rock star**. (F)

Discussion, Part 2 Answer Key – Possible Occupations

1. babysitter, nanny, teacher, pediatrician, psychologist, nurse
2. police officer, fire fighter, waiter, nurse, doctor, guard, military personnel
3. police officer, fire fighter, electric wire installer, lumberjack, pilot, construction laborer
4. chef, waiter, (server), host/hostess, dishwasher, janitor
5. doctor, nurse, aide, administrator, assistant, technician, janitor

Looking for a Job

Prediction dictation page 90 CD Track 49

Sara Soto has two children ages seven and twelve. She wants **to** find a part-time job while **her** children are in school. **She** doesn't want to work on weekends or **during** the summer.

First, **she** thinks about what she can do. **Second**, she thinks about what she likes **to** do. She likes to drive, **and** she thinks she **can** get a special driver's **license** to drive a school bus. This way she can work while her **children** are in school.

To apply for this **type** of job, she can call **the** superintendent's office of the **San** Antonio Public Schools or a school system in a nearby town and ask if there **are** any openings for school bus drivers. She **can** ask about the qualifications **and** training, too. What are some other ways that Sara can **find** a part-time job?

Social Security

Prediction dictation   page 93   CD Track 50

Everyone in the United **States** who works has **a** Social Security card and **a** Social Security number. Your employer takes money out of your paycheck and gives it **to** the government. You get money back when you **retire**, or **when** you are too sick **to** work.

To get **a** card and **a** number, go **to** a Social Security Office and fill out a form. Call the **office** or go on the Internet (Social Security. Org) to see what you need to bring with **you**.   For example, you may need to bring a passport, a birth certificate, or a Green **Card**.

Listening   page 94

Voice:	Please hold. All of our representatives are busy. Your call is important to us. Someone will be with you shortly.
Representative:	Hello, Social Security. How can I help you?
Francisco:	Hello. My name is Francisco Maronni. I need a Social Security Card and a Social Security number. What should I bring with me?
Representative:	Were you born in the United States?
Francisco:	No, I was born in Italy.
Representative:	Are you an American citizen?
Francisco:	No, I'm not.
Representative:	Then you must bring a U.S. Immigration Form or an Alien Registration Card. That's a Green Card.
Francisco:	How much will it cost?
Representative:	There is no charge. It's free.
Francisco:	Thank you.

Answers
1. Yes, he has to wait.
2. He wants to know what he has to bring with him.
3. Were you born in the USA? Are you a citizen?
4. He was born in Italy.
5. He must bring his Green Card.
6. There is no charge.

The Pay Slip

Partial dictation page 96 CD Track 51

Frank is **19**. He is **very happy**. Jobs are not easy **to find**, but he has a **job**. He **is working** for a company that **makes** furniture.

Every **week** he gets **a check** for $480, or more if **he works** overtime. He also gets a statement of earnings and deductions. **It is** important for him to keep this.

He is going **to work** full-time for **fifteen months**. He is saving **his money** so **he can go** to community college.

Answers page 97

1. $12.00
2. $18.00
3. 45
4. $570.00
5. $408.30
6. $34.20
7. $57.00
8. $28.50
9. $42.00
10. $161.70

Banks and Bank Accounts

Partial dictation   page 100   CD Track 52

If you **work**, it is important **to open** a checking account **at a bank**. Most employers will **put** your salary **into** your **bank** account by direct deposit.

You **can** withdraw money by writing a check, by using a **bank** debit **card**, or by using an **ATM**. If you **need to buy** a large item like a **car**, you may **go** to your **bank** to get a loan.

Listening   page 101

Bank Employee:	Good morning. Can I help you?
Student:	Yes, I'd like to open a bank account.
Bank Employee:	Do you want to open a checking account or a savings account?
Student:	Both.
Bank Employee:	Do you have two pieces of ID? One of them must have a picture of you on it.
Student:	Yes, I have two IDs with pictures. One is my passport. The other is my Student ID. I also have a credit card from my bank in Mexico.
Bank Employee:	That's perfect. All of our bank officers are busy now, but someone can be with you in about 20 minutes or sooner. Please sit over here.
Student:	Thank you very much.
Bank Employee:	While you're waiting, you can begin to fill out the top part of this form.

Answers   b, c, b, c, a

Writing Checks

Partial dictation   page 102   CD Track 53

Henry **and his wife** Maryanne both **work**. At the end of **the month** their employers **put money** into their joint checking account by direct deposit.

They **use** their credit cards **for many things** they buy **in stores**. At the end of every month, **they sit down** together to write checks **for** their other bills. These are **some** of the checks they write **every month**: the gas company, the electric company, the rent, and medical bills. **They are** very careful to write down the amount of **every check** in their checkbook.

Henry Drives to Work

Vocabulary Part 3   page 104   CD Track 54

1. windshield wipers
2. headlights
3. ignition key
4. gas pedal
5. brake
6. speedometer

Partial dictation   page 105   CD Track 54

Henry is a **very good** driver. When he **gets into** his car, he **puts on** his seatbelt. He puts **his key** into the ignition and **starts** the car. It is raining, so he **turns on** the windshield wipers. It is almost dark so he **turns on** the headlights. He **puts his foot** on the gas pedal and begins to drive to his night job at the hospital. Soon he comes to a **stop** sign. He **puts his foot** on the brake and **stops the car**. In **five** minutes he is at the hospital and **parks the car** in the parking lot. Henry **works** in the emergency room in the hospital, and sometimes he has **to work** at night.

Fifty Minutes on the Road

Partial dictation   page 107   CD Track 55
Dictation 1

Fifty minutes **is** the average total **time** an American worker travels from **home** to **work** every day. Most people drive. Some **people** ride their bicycles. Others take a **bus** or train.

Listen and Write   (Read down, under 55 first)

How Americans get to work

	under 55	over 55
Car	76.6	78.7
Carpool	9.7	7. 3
Public transportation	4.9	4.0
Walk	2.8	2.3
Taxi, etc.	1.7	1.3
Work at home	4.3	6.4

Discussion Check

1. 6.4%
2. 4.9%
3. 2.3%
4. 1.3%
5. 9.7%

Dictation 2   page 108

What do we do on our way **to work**? 96% (ninety-six percent) say that they **talk** to other passengers. **74%** say that they **eat** their breakfast or **drink** coffee or tea. **51%** use a **cell phone**, and **19%** say they sometimes **comb** their **hair** or **put on** lipstick. Some people listen to **music** or the news.

Henry's Accident

Partial dictation   page 109   CD Track 56

Henry is driving **to his job** at the hospital. He **sees** the **stop** sign. He **puts his foot** on the brake pedal and stops. The car behind him **hits his car**. Henry has his seatbelt on and he is **not hurt**.

Both cars go to the side **of the road**. A woman **gets out of** her car and says she is sorry. She says, "It is my fault." No one **is hurt**.

1. They call the **police.**
2. They give each other their **phone** numbers. (618-233-**5768** and 618-377-**2314**)
3. They give each other their **license** information.
4. They give each other the **names** of their insurance companies.
5. They give each other information on their **car** registration papers.
6. Then they wait for the **police**.

How to Get a Driver's License

Prediction dictation   page 112   CD Track 57

What should you do? First go to the Registry of Motor Vehicles **and** get a Driver's Handbook. Study the laws **in** the **handbook**. When you are ready to take the written **test**, go back to the RMV and take **it**. If you pass the **test**, you will get a learner's permit. You will also have a vision **test** and a road sign test.

If you **are** a new driver, you must practice a lot. There must always be a licensed driver **in the** car with **you**. Some people go **to** driving schools. When you think **you** are ready for a road **test**, make an appointment to take **it**. If you don't pass the **road** test, you can take **it** again. After you pass the **road** test, the Registry of Motor Vehicles will mail your license to **you**.

Listening   page 112

Two friends are talking.

Carole: Hi Pat. How are you?

Pat: I'm very nervous. I'm taking the written test for my driver's license today.

Carole: That's no big deal. Remember to bring something that shows when you were born. Also bring something that you have signed, so they can see what your writing looks like. Remember to bring something with your address on it, so they can see where you live. Also don't forget the $30.00.

Pat: I have all of that ready.

Carole: Do you wear glasses sometimes?

Pat: Yes.

Carole: Be sure to bring them, because they're going to test your vision. Can you drive?

Pat: Yes. But I haven't driven in ten years. I'm going to take driving lessons at a driving school as soon as I pass the written test.

Answers Do not check $100.00 and a photo ID.

Road Signs

Dictogloss   page 113   CD Track 58

1. You can't park here.
2. School children are crossing the street.
3. There is a hospital to your right.

Listening   page 114

Tic Tac Toe/BINGO game

In random order, recite the words in the box. Check them off as you read them, so that when someone cries "BINGO," you can verify their answers.

stop	one way	no trucks	hospital
left turn only	railroad	no passing zone	do not enter
dead end	speed limit 60	toll ahead $1.00	slow